CW01430461

Schools Council
Research Studies

Ability and Examinations at 16+

Other books in this series

Schools Council
Research Studies

Ability and Examinations at 16+

Barbara A. Bloomfield
John L. Dobby
Lesley Kendall

Examinations and Tests Research Unit
National Foundation for Educational Research
in England and Wales

M

Macmillan Education

First published 1979

Published by
MACMILLAN EDUCATION LTD
Houndmills Basingstoke Hampshire RG21 2XS
and London
Associated companies in Delhi Dublin
Hong Kong Johannesburg Lagos Melbourne
New York Singapore and Tokyo

Filmset by BAS Printers Limited, Over Wallop, Hampshire
Printed in Hong Kong

British Library Cataloguing in Publication Data
Bloomfield, Barbara
Ability and examinations at 16+. – (Schools Council.
Research studies ISSN 0306-0292).
1. Certificate of secondary education examination
(Great Britain) – Statistics 2. General certificate
of education examination (Great Britain) – Statistics
I. Title   II. Dobby, John   III. Kendall, Lesley
IV. Series
373.1′2′64   LB3056.G7

ISBN 0-333-26319-7

Contents

Tables and figure

Figure

Acknowledgements

We are particularly indebted to teachers and pupils in the schools included in this study. Without their co-operation in what was for them a very onerous task the study would not have been possible. We also wish to thank the examining boards for providing us with the 1974 examination results sheets so that we were able to record the subjects entered by each candidate.

Our thanks are also due to colleagues in the NFER, to:

Dr A. S. Willmott, the Principal Research Officer in charge of the Examinations and Tests Research Unit (ETRU) at the NFER who supervised the study and offered his constant support.

The Statistics Section at the NFER who spent long hours, including evenings and weekends, on the mammoth task of processing the data which were collected.

Linda Sargeant who persevered with the typing of the several drafts and also typed the final version of the report.

Finally the Schools Council must be thanked for sponsoring the work of the ETRU and therefore for making the work possible.

The excerpt from 'An Analysis of GCE and CSE Examinations Grades' by A. S. Willmott is reproduced in Appendix A by kind permission of the author.

Preface

In the 1973/74 school year, and until Easter 1974, for the first time the whole 16-year-old population was, truancy apart, in school. This event is already well enshrined in our educational past and those unfortunately dubbed 'RoSLA children' are rarely heard of today.

Prior to Easter 1974, however, the Examinations and Tests Research Unit (ETRU) had been preparing the ground for a substantial study which was aimed, on the one hand, at eliciting which subjects and sectors the candidate entries were being distributed among and, on the other, at investigating whether the examination boards were able to maintain examination standards in the face of an expected rise in subject entries following the raising of the school leaving age. (The rise in subject entries from 1973 to 1974 was actually 5·3% in the GCE sector and 52·8% in the CSE sector.) The part of this joint study—fully entitled the '1974 Comparability/Range of Ability Study'—dealing with the candidate entries to specific subjects is presented here; the comparability aspect is reported elsewhere (Willmott and Bloomfield, 1977).

That there was felt to be the need for a range of ability study underlines the fact that relatively little was known at a national level about candidate entries across sectors. It was not known, for example, what proportion of the whole 16-year-old group sat for English or mathematics in either the GCE or CSE sectors. We now know that the figures are 82% and 72% respectively, but because of the ever increasing overlap between the two examination sectors (see Table 4.3 and discussion) it was not possible to determine these figures without a special study such as that reported here.

The examination load on some candidates is considerable and this report helps to put into perspective the rationale for a single system of examining at 16+. Barbara Bloomfield had the unenviable task of keeping track of candidate entries and the general administration of the exercise while John Dobby spent long hours collating the various results and presenting them in a simple form. Our project statistician, Lesley Kendall, played a central role in producing the analyses, and much of the detailed programming and data handling as well as theoretical design fell on her shoulders. It is thus fitting that she should have had a part in preparing this report at the end of the project.

Many of the results were produced to allow the Schools Council to evaluate the range of ability of candidates entering for the 16+ feasibility study exercises and the distribution of reference test scores of candidates by subject of entry were made available to the examination boards in 1975. What follows is a detailed description of the procedure used and a general summary of the main results for a wider audience.

Finally, for easy reference, on page 199 there is a list of the reports produced by the Examinations and Tests Research Unit of the National Foundation for Educational Research since its inception in 1964.

Alan S. Wilmott
Principal Research Officer
Examinations and Tests Research Unit

1 Introduction

Background to the study

The Examinations and Tests Research Unit (ETRU) of the National Foundation for Educational Research (NFER) has been engaged in research in the field of examinations on behalf of the Schools Council since 1964. Its activities have included the investigation of the comparability of grading standards in the Certificate of Secondary Education (CSE) examinations from 1965 to 1968 and in both CSE and the General Certificate of Education (GCE) O-level examinations from 1973 to 1975. Comparisons have been made between grading standards in different years, subjects, examining boards and modes. Other aspects of the examinations such as their reliability, the effect of pupils having to make a choice of questions and the usage of continuous assessment in the CSE have also been studied. The investigation described in the present report arose from two important developments in the field of education: raising the school leaving age from 15 to 16 in 1972 and proposals to introduce a common examination system for 16-year-old pupils to replace the existing GCE O-level and CSE systems.

The regulations which raised the minimum leaving age from 15 to 16 were implemented from September 1972 and affected all children who had not reached their fifteenth birthday by that date. Under these new arrangements children whose sixteenth birthday fell in the period 1 September 1973 to 31 January 1974 inclusive were required to remain at school until the following Easter, and those whose sixteenth birthday fell in the period 1 February 1974 to 31 August 1974 had to remain at school until the end of the summer term. As a result, in the school year beginning September 1973 all children whose sixteenth birthday fell in that year were in school until Easter and many of them until the end of the summer term 1974. The whole group of these pupils make up what is referred to in this report as the '16+ age group'. The majority of these pupils were in their fifth year of secondary education, the year in which the CSE and GCE O-level examinations are usually taken.

The regulations of the CSE examination require that candidates attending schools must be in the final term of the fifth year of a course of

1

secondary education or have completed such a course and be aged at least 16 on 1 September of the calendar year of their examinations (or, exceptionally, may be 15 years 6 months on that date). Some GCE O-level examinations are usually taken by pupils at a similar age although they can, in fact, be taken at any age. The Department of Education and Science requires that a candidate for GCE O-level

who is not at least sixteen years of age on 1 September in the year of examination may not be entered unless:

> (a) he has completed or is about to complete a five-year course of secondary education, or
> (b) his head teacher certifies both that it is educationally desirable for him to take the examination and that he has pursued a course of study with such a degree of competence as to make it very probable that he will pass in the subject(s) offered.
> (Joint Matriculation Board, 1974, p 6)

In practice the entry of younger candidates for the GCE O-level examinations before the fifth year of secondary education is not uncommon.

Both the CSE and GCE O-level examinations are, therefore, intended primarily for 16-year-old pupils. The two systems exist side by side as a result of the historical development of public examinations since the nineteenth century and, more specifically, since the introduction of the GCE O-level examinations in 1951. A report by the Secondary School Examinations Council (SSEC), the forerunner of the Schools Council, traces the developments leading to the establishment of the CSE examinations in 1965 (Secondary School Examinations Council, 1963, pp 98–100). The GCE O-level examination was designed on a single subject basis primarily for those completing a five-year course in selective secondary schools. The CSE examination was established, following the recommendations of a subcommittee of the SSEC under Robert Beloe, as a subject examination organized on a regional basis, under the control of teachers. The ability range of would-be candidates was made explicit by Beloe.

We have assumed that up to 20 per cent of the total 16-year-old age group may be expected to attempt (though not necessarily to pass) GCE O-level in a fair range of subjects, say four or more. We think that candidates in the next 20 per cent of the age group might take the examinations in a fair spread of subjects, say four or five (unless they were simultaneously attempting particular subjects in the GCE) and that the standard of the papers set and the marking should be such that a substantial majority of pupils within this group might expect, without undue pressure, to obtain passes in this range of subjects. We think that candidates within a range up to about the next 20 per cent of the age group who are those round about the average of ability, might attempt and often secure passes in, fewer subjects. (Secondary School Examinations Council, 1963, p 111)

The SSEC, in its *Seventh Report*, accepted that the Beloe report had correctly defined the scope of the examination and proposed that:

(1) the CSE system of examinations should be designed for a band of candidates extending from those who just overlap the group taking the ordinary level of the GCE examination, to those who are just below the average in ability;

(2) the above definition of the scope of the examinations should not, however, be interpreted too rigorously. There will be some pupils whose ability in a particular subject would justify their entering for the examination, although their general ability falls outside the band we have defined. And the converse is equally true: some pupils whose general ability is within the band we have defined would be ill-advised to enter for some subjects. (Secondary School Examinations Council, 1963, pp 121–122)

Thus developed two systems which currently function side by side and aim overall to provide examinations for roughly the top 60% of 16-year-old pupils. Willmott (1975) has shown in his study of candidates in the 1968 and 1973 examinations that the practice of entering candidates in both the CSE and GCE sectors was very common. Over 40% of the candidates in the sample took at least one CSE examination and one GCE examination. Of these dual entry candidates 12·5% were double entry candidates i.e. they had entered for the *same* subject in each sector. This problem of identifying the most suitable examination for pupils on the borderline of the two examinations led to increasing pressure for a single examination system. Developmental work in connexion with the possible introduction of a common system of examining began in 1970 and a number of feasibility studies were initiated in certain subjects by consortia of GCE and CSE examining boards. The purpose of these studies was to explore ways of devising examination papers and other assessment materials which would be suitable for the full range of ability of candidates currently entering for the CSE and GCE O-level examinations. Examinations Bulletin 23, *A Common System of Examining at 16+* (Schools Council, 1971), defined the range for a particular subject as stretching from the 40th to the 100th percentile of the whole 16+ age group and thus reiterated the intended ability range of the examination system at 16+ contained in the SSEC's proposals described earlier in the section. In 1974 there were over 68,000 subject entries for trial examinations being developed in the common examination feasibility studies. These examinations were also 'live' in the sense that candidates who achieved the required standard were awarded the normal CSE and GCE O-level certificates. It was essential, therefore, that there should be some means of comparing the ability of candidates entered for them against that of candidates entered for the normal board examinations.

Evidence concerning the ability range of examination candidates in the GCE and CSE sectors in the individual boards and in the subjects concerned, as well as nationally, was necessary for the conduct of these studies.

Some information was available about the ability of examination candidates before 1974. For example, in his study of candidates for the 1968 and 1973 examinations, Willmott (1975) showed that there was in fact a considerable overlap in the ability (as measured by a general reference test) of CSE and GCE O-level candidates. In 1973, however, as in previous years many pupils in the 16+ age group did not remain in school to complete the full five years of secondary education and were therefore not candidates for the examinations. In the school year beginning September 1973 the whole 16+ age group was legally bound to remain at school at least until Easter 1974 and a rise in the number of examination entries was expected, particularly in the CSE sector. It was also predicted that a large proportion of these new candidates would be at the lower end of the ability range, making it necessary for the examining boards to award more of the lower grades. Prior to 1974 there had been considerable variations across the regions of England and Wales in the proportion of pupils staying on at school beyond the statutory leaving age. Table 1.1 gives the proportions in maintained schools over six regions of England and Wales in 1972 and 1973, and the most striking

Table 1.1   Percentage* of pupils remaining at maintained schools beyond the statutory leaving age by region 1972 and 1973

Region	Pupils aged 15**		Pupils aged 16**	
	1972	1973	1972	1973
North	51·3	51·2	29·1	28·7
Yorks and Humberside	51·6	52·4	31·1	30·4
North west	52·3	53·0	28·7	28·6
East midlands	51·8	53·5	29·8	29·5
West midlands	56·0	56·2	31·4	31·7
East Anglia	52·6	55·0	29·3	28·8
South east	66·2	66·7	40·8	40·7
South west	63·5	63·9	34·4	33·5
Wales	54·3	54·8	37·1	36·1
Total	58·0	58·6	34·3	34·0

*Expressed as percentage of 13-year-old pupils two and three years earlier
** Age at beginning of January
(Taken from *DES Statistics of Education*, Volume I, Table 10, 1974)

feature is the larger proportion of pupils who stayed at school in the south east and south west of England compared with the rest of the country. Since the CSE examinations are organized on a regional basis, the effect of raising the school leaving age was unlikely to be felt uniformly by the fourteen regionally organized CSE examining boards and the maintenance of grading standards, given new candidates of largely unknown calibre in individual subjects, gave cause for concern.

Overall responsibility for standards in the examinations and for work concerned with the feasibility of introducing a common examination for 16-year-old pupils lay with the Schools Council. Although raising the school leaving age presented problems to the examining boards, it provided in 1974 the first opportunity of investigating the ability of the whole 16+ age group and of comparing the range of ability of CSE, GCE O-level and non-examination candidates.

Aims of the study

The Schools Council commissioned the Examinations and Tests Research Unit to carry out a global study in 1974 to investigate various issues arising from the developments described in the previous section. The aims of the research reported herein may be summarized as:

1 To investigate the range and distribution of ability of candidates from the 16+ age group entered for the CSE and GCE O-level examination in relation to the whole 16+ age group both nationally and regionally.
2 To estimate the proportion of the 16+ age group entering CSE and GCE O-level examinations in the major subjects nationally and regionally.
3 To provide evidence in the form of national norms for the feasibility studies for a common examination system.

In addition, two further aspects of the public examinations system at 16+ were to be studied, namely:

4 To investigate comparability of standards in the CSE and GCE O-level examinations subject by subject across years and boards.
5 To relate the standard of the CSE grade 4 to the distribution of ability of the 16+ age group.

The last two aims are the subject of another report (Willmott and Bloomfield, 1977). Aims 1–3 were to be fulfilled by the administration of a general reference test and by the production of norms in the form of distributions of test scores with means and standard deviations, for the sub-groups of interest among the 16+ age group. These were to be submitted to the Schools Council and the examining boards by April 1975 for the evaluation of the common examination feasibility studies.

Ability

The problem of studying ability is difficult to solve satisfactorily. It may be argued that, for the purpose of studying the ability of candidates in individual subjects, a test designed to measure ability in that subject is required. This, however, would not solve the problems posed in the study described here since pupils who were not entering examinations were of interest, and comparisons across subjects were to be made. Indeed, it would be difficult to construct a test in a particular subject, to make comparisons across boards, since there are considerable differences between the syllabuses of the various CSE and GCE examining boards and of schools entering candidates in Mode III.

An alternative is a test of general ability. As we have seen on page 3, the SSEC in its *Seventh Report* used the term ability primarily to refer to general ability which is normally distributed across an age group, although the SSEC also accepted that candidates' ability in a particular subject, especially in cases in which candidates enter the examination in a single subject only, may be higher than their general ability.

The problem of defining general ability remains. It is commonly accepted that general ability of this kind can only be measured and defined in operational terms by means of intelligence tests and general aptitude tests which have been validated by procedures such as factor analysis. Hall (1977) distinguishes between the terms 'general intelligence', 'general educational ability' and 'general scholastic ability' which he points out are commonly used to describe essentially the same thing. He, on the other hand, defines 'general intelligence'

... as 'general, cognitive, ability' which is manifested by an individual's capacity to carry out 'good reasoning', that is, reasoning which is selective and relevant to the individual's own needs and goals. This view is presented not as a conclusive or comprehensive definition but rather as a description highlighting certain key words and phrases.

General educational ability is presented as a complex ability underlying performance in varying degrees in virtually all subject examinations. Using Vernon's model of the structure of educational abilities, this ability is seen as comprising general intelligence ('g'), standard educational skills ('$v:ed$') and a complex of non-cognitive factors ('X' etc.) which combine and interact to influence performance in nearly all branches of all subjects.

The third concept, general scholastic ability, is presented largely as an operational refinement of the concept of general educational ability. Whereas general educational ability relates to a common ability underlying examination performance, general scholastic ability relates to the complex of skills influencing performance on tests of scholastic ability. The essential distinguishing characteristic, in terms of Vernon's model, is that performance on tests of scholastic ability is unlikely to involve to the same degree the complex of non-cognitive factors which underlie examination performance; such tests are less likely to relate to the pupils' aspirations, interests, preparations and motivations.

The concluding comment in this chapter is left to Butcher (1968) from a discussion of the concept of intelligence; the comment applies equally to the other concepts discussed in this chapter.

' "Intelligence" is a noun, and nouns often refer to things or objects. Even when we know perfectly well that intelligence is not a "thing", but a sophisticated abstraction from behaviour, we may sometimes half-consciously endow it with a kind of shadowy existence distinct and separate from the intelligent organisms which alone give it meaning, or, more insidiously, think it is a "thing" that these organisms "have", rather than a description of the way they behave.'
(Hall, 1977, pp 38–39)

It may be argued that a pragmatic approach to an investigation of the ability of the 16+ age group lies through a test designed to measure general educational ability and defined in operational terms as a test of general scholastic ability. Such a test, Test 100, had been used in the NFER's comparability studies carried out in 1968 and 1973. Willmott (1975) traces the development of Test 100 and discusses its operational characteristics and validity in 'An Analysis of GCE and CSE Examination Grades'. The relevant section is reproduced in full in Appendix A and summarized below.

Test 100 is a fifty-minute test composed of 80 multiple-choice questions, mostly of the five-choice type and exactly half the items are designed to measure verbal ability and the other half mathematical quantitative ability. (See App. A p 65). Willmott comes to the conclusion that Test 100 appears satisfactory in its operational characteristics. Its reliability, derived from internal consistency estimates, was 0·92 and 0·93 in 1968 and 1973 respectively and it discriminated between candidates in secondary schools taking public examinations in 1968 and 1973.

Willmott also concludes that the relationship of Test 100 with performance in the CSE and GCE O-level examinations is reasonable especially in the 'academic' subjects; the highest correlation being for mathematics (0·65 and 0·61 in CSE and GCE respectively). The lower correlations for French (0·26 and 0·36) and history (0·36 and 0·35) may be partly explained by the fact that these subjects are often in the school timetable as subject options. Pupils' ability in a particular subject, as perceived by themselves or their teachers, will influence choice of subjects. (The more restricted the range of ability, the lower the correlations will be.) The lower correlation may also be partly explained by the presence of specific subject factors other than the more general ones of Test 100. It may be argued for example that history as examined at the 16+ age group level requires an ability to memorize facts, a skill which is not necessarily called for in a general scholastic ability test.

Correlations with 'non-academic' subjects such as art are lower, presumably because of specific subject factors being present to a greater extent. The size of the correlations must also be seen in the context of the limits set by the reliability of both the test and the criteria so that a correlation higher than about 0·8 is unlikely to occur.

Willmott (1975) draws attention to two possible flaws in Test 100: there appears to be an overall bias in favour of boys because, although there is a slight bias towards girls on verbal items there is a stronger bias towards boys on quantitative items. Possible bias has to be borne in mind, therefore, when the sexes are considered relatively or common scores are used. For example, if 'ability' is understood to mean performance in a particular subject examination, then girls may appear of higher ability than boys with equivalent Test 100 scores. If, on the other hand, ability is interpreted from scores obtained on Test 100, the boys may appear to be of higher ability than girls with equivalent subject examination grades.

Evidence such as that summarized above supported the view that, in the context of an investigation into the range of ability of examination candidates within the 16 + age group, Test 100 was a reasonably valid measure of general scholastic ability and a reliable measure for use in the study. In addition, in the context of the NFER's overall research brief, which included comparability studies of the 1974 examinations, the choice of Test 100 provided continuity with the 1968 and 1973 comparability studies. Thus it was possible to combine both aspects of the research, the range of ability as outlined in aims 1–3 above and the comparability aspect (aims 4 and 5).

Outline of this report

The decision of the Schools Council to cover all aspects of both the comparability studies and the investigation of the ability of the 16 + age group in one operation required an extensive research design and this is described in Chapter 2.

In Chapter 3 the way in which the information was collected and handled is reported and it includes a precise description of the subjects under scrutiny. It draws attention to the variety of syllabuses and the difficulty of defining a subject. Chapter 3 also describes the sample of schools and candidates including some data on the sample schools' pattern of entries to the GCE examination boards. Estimates of the population made from the sample data and an appraisal of different methods of making these estimates follow and the chapter closes with further information on Test 100 derived from data from the present study.

In Chapter 4 is presented a summary of the results of the study which were submitted in the form of norms (i.e. distributions of Test 100 scores) to the Schools Council and the CSE and GCE examining boards in April 1975 for the evaluation of the common examination feasibility studies. The results are summarized in the present report in the form of estimates of the number and proportion of all pupils in the 16+ age group having entries for certain examinations together with their mean and standard deviation of Test 100 scores. These estimates are reported in Chapter 4 for the whole 16+ age group, for all examination candidates and for sub-groups of candidates. These sub-groups include all CSE candidates, all GCE candidates, all candidates entering at least one examination in either sector and in both sectors; for each major subject all candidates entering in each sector and both sectors and in each board; for each board all candidates entering in all subjects and each major subject. A full description of these sub-groups is given at the beginning of Chapter 4 for ease of reference. All the estimates are given for boys and girls separately and for both together.

This report is concluded in Chapter 5 with a brief summary of the most striking features revealed by the investigation and a discussion of some of the issues.

2 The design of the study

Introduction

As was described in Chapter 1 the focus of the study was the 16+ age group in schools (excluding special schools) in England and Wales in 1974 and the 16+ age group was defined as all pupils whose sixteenth birthday fell between 1 September 1973 and 31 August 1974 inclusive. The majority of these pupils, but not all, were in the fifth year of secondary education and were entering CSE and GCE O-level examinations in the summer of 1974. Some able pupils, however, were 'accelerated' so that they were in the sixth form in the year of the study and had taken GCE O-level examinations a year or even two years earlier. Pupils who were entering GCE O-level examinations in most of their subjects in their sixteenth year may also have taken the examination in one or two subjects the previous year.

This led to a problem of definition of 'examinations entered by the 16+ age group'. Considering strictly the examinations entered by the 16+ age group in the year in which they became 16 would have reduced the apparent range of ability of GCE candidates, especially in English language, mathematics and French, since many able candidates may have taken these subjects a year earlier. Only in very exceptional circumstances would this occur in the case of the CSE examinations. To ensure valid comparisons between the CSE and GCE sectors, therefore, it was necessary to consider all CSE and GCE O-level examinations entered up to and including Summer 1974. It should be noted that all entries recorded by the boards were included even if the candidate was absent for the examination itself.

Willmott (1975) showed that the existence of the CSE and GCE O-level examinations side by side led to the practice of pupils entering examinations in both the CSE and GCE sectors in the same year: pupils enter either different subjects in each sector ('dual entry') or the same subject in both sectors ('double entry'). The reasons for dual and double entries are probably varied and sometimes complex, but in designing the present study it was necessary to recognize their existence.

Pupils can, therefore, be categorized as follows. First there are those pupils who do not enter any GCE or CSE examinations. Then there are the pupils who may be designated examination entrants which, for the purpose of this study, means all pupils entering for at least one GCE or CSE examination. This second group may be further subdivided into GCE candidates (all pupils entering at least one GCE examination) and CSE candidates (all those entering at least one CSE examination). It will be realized that these last two categories have pupils in common, wherever a pupil enters at least one CSE examination *and* at least one GCE examination. Similarly it is possible to look at all pupils taking a given subject, regardless of whether their entry is in the CSE or GCE sector and then at all pupils taking that subject in the GCE sector and all pupils taking it in the CSE sector.

The problems for the design of this study which were posed by the practice of dual and double entries were increased by the variety of syllabuses provided by the boards. Syllabuses covering similar content areas were found with different titles and those with the same title sometimes varied considerably in their content. A coding system was necessary which would enable a subject to be generally recognized and all sylabuses included in each subject identified. The way in which this was done is described in Chapter 3.

The design

SAMPLING

The 1973/4 16+ age group in England and Wales, comprised approximately 650 000 pupils and, ideally, a random sample of these pupils should have been studied. However, this would have been very difficult to obtain since it would have involved pupils in a very large number of schools. Instead, a sample of schools was chosen and all pupils in the 16+ age group within these schools were given Test 100.

Since one aspect of the study was to investigate examination entries, not only for England and Wales as a whole but also for individual CSE and GCE boards, it was necessary to obtain samples of adequate size from each board. The fourteen CSE boards are organized on a regional basis, and a school may enter candidates only for the CSE board covering the appropriate region. The GCE sector does not have a regional structure and, within certain limitations, a pupil can enter GCE examinations under any of the eight GCE boards. It is thus more difficult to ensure that the sample of entries to a GCE board is representative. However, a procedure which ensures that the national sample is representative of the age group should also ensure that any sub-group of the 16+ age group is correctly represented in the total.

A sample of schools was drawn separately for each CSE region. It would have been possible to take the same proportion of schools in each region, but a proportion sufficient to give an adequate number of schools in the smallest region would have given a sample many times larger than necessary in the bigger regions. Previous work had indicated that about 20 schools were needed in each region to give a sufficient range of types and sizes of school. A sample of this size was, therefore, taken from each CSE region and resulted in 1 in 8 schools being selected in the smallest region and 1 in 30 schools in the biggest.

The main disadvantage of such a sampling scheme is that the national picture cannot be obtained simply by adding together the results for each CSE region. Rather, each board must contribute to the total in proportion to its size so that, for example, a region with 400 schools will have twice the weight in the national picture as a region with 200 schools, even though the size of the sample is the same for each region. As the sample of schools in each region is selected to be representative and because national results are obtained on a weighted basis, a representative sample of pupils in the 16+ age group is in effect obtained. (See Appendix B for the technical details of this procedure.)

CANDIDATE OR SUBJECT ENTRIES

An aim of the study was to investigate what proportion of the 16+ age group entered at least one GCE or CSE examination at any time up to and including summer 1974, and for that purpose interest lay in candidate numbers and not in subject entries. On the other hand, information was also required on candidates entering a particular subject and, in that sense, interest lay in subject entries. It was therefore necessary to record every subject entry. However, depending on the purpose for which records would be used, there were two possible bases for calculating the results. A candidate could be included once if he had entered the subject only in the CSE sector or only in the GCE sector and twice if he had entered the subject in both sectors. Alternatively, a candidate could be included once if he had entered in the GCE sector only, in the CSE sector only, or if he had entered in both sectors. One of the reasons for looking at subjects was to estimate the range of ability for which a single examination would have to be designed if a common examining system at 16+ were to be introduced. In such a situation, of course, there would be no question of one candidate having two entries in the same subject. It is perhaps a reasonable assumption that candidates entering the same subject in both sectors are likely to be neither particularly weak nor particularly able. If this is so, distributions of ability based on entries would tend to be more 'humped' at the middle levels of ability than would be the case under a common system of examinations.

A candidate may have been recorded as having entered the same subject twice not only because he has entered once in each sector but also because he or she may have entered:

(a) the same subject in two different GCE boards.
(b) the same subject on two separate occasions, once prior to Summer 1974 and once in Summer 1974. These two entries might be in the same or different boards or sectors.
(c) a 'double subject', for example, an English examination covering both literature and language aspects and designed to carry twice the weight of other subjects.
(d) two separate subjects which were grouped together for the evaluation of the common examination feasibility studies. An example of this was housecraft, and will be described more fully in Chapter 3.

It was eventually decided that the most sensible solution would be to include a candidate once only in any group of candidates being studied so that the range of ability for each group could be calculated on the basis of candidate ability regardless of the number of subject entries.

EARLY ENTRIES

Candidates who had entered an examination prior to summer 1974 gave details of the subject and the sector. They were not asked for the name of the board since this was likely to be unknown or unreliable. This caused no difficulty with CSE entries, because the number of pupils involved was very small and, in any case, it could be assumed that in general the board was determined by the region to which the candidate belonged. There may have been occasions on which this was not so as, for example, in the case of a pupil moving a few months prior to the testing. However, it was felt that this was likely to be a sufficiently rare occurence to occur only within a very small proportion of the 16+ age group, and could thus be ignored.

In the GCE sector, the situation was made much more complex by the various patterns of entry described earlier. It was not easy, therefore, to identify the boards used by the candidates who had entered examinations prior to 1974. This did not matter when considering results for the whole GCE sector or for the combined CSE/GCE sector. It did, however, affect results within a GCE board. As there was no way of assigning GCE early entries to boards, it seemed that these results would have to be omitted from the board-by-board analyses. This, however, would have led to difficulties in making comparisons with entries in the CSE sector. Omitting early entries in the GCE sector was likely to result in a disproportionate loss of high-ability candidates since these pupils were those most likely to have taken one or more GCE examinations before they reached the age of 16.

It was decided to overcome this problem by giving Test 100 to all those pupils in the sample schools who were younger than the 16+ age group but who were entering at least one GCE examination in the summer of 1974. Thus results within a GCE board did not include the early entries of the 1974 16+ age group, but included entries by younger candidates in summer 1974. This matching process may not have been exact. It assumed that the pattern of early entries remained much the same from year to year, an assumption which may not have been valid if, for instance, a school was in the process of reorganization from selective to comprehensive intake or if there had been a recent change in school staff. Additionally, some of the 16+ age group may have entered a subject prior to summer 1974 but were taking that subject again in summer 1974. However, as explained earlier, in this case they were included only once for that subject. Nevertheless, substituting the entries of young candidates for the early entries of 16+ pupils was likely to lead to a slight overestimate of the number of pupils attempting a given subject at any time up to the summer of their sixteenth year. The number of such cases was not likely to be so large as to make this a serious problem and indeed could only affect the results for individual GCE boards.

More serious was the effect of age on scores on Test 100. Many of the tests used in educational measurement show a tendency for scores to be higher for older groups of pupils, although this effect normally levels off by the mid-teens. However, there was a possibility that the inclusion of test scores of young candidates would give lower mean scores on Test 100 than would be the case if only the 16+ age group were to be considered. It was therefore necessary to check whether or not there was a significant age effect in Test 100, so that the observed scores of young candidates could be adjusted if necessary to give an estimate of the score which would be obtained a year later. Assuming that young entrants have roughly the same age distribution, with the difference only of a year, as that section of the 16+ age group who entered at least one GCE early, the effect of correcting for age would give an accurate estimate of the Test 100 scores which would be observed if such early entries were included instead of the entries from young candidates. A description of the method of estimating this age effect is given in Appendix B.

Calculation of main results

The data were to be analysed on the NFER's IBM 1130 computer. This is a small machine by modern standards, and thus imposed certain limitations on the way the required analyses could be carried out. The most important restriction was that it was not possible to handle the whole sample, amounting to over 30 000 pupils, together. For most of the results required, the easiest approach was to divide the data into sections, a section for each board. This was easily done for the fourteen CSE boards because of the regional structure. Each pupil's data included the CSE region to which his or her school belonged, regardless of whether the individual pupil or even the school entered for any CSE examinations. Hence a section of data defined by one particular CSE region code contained all the pupils who took at least one CSE in the board, no pupils taking any other CSE board, and a number of pupils taking no CSE subjects. Because of the overlap in entry to the GCE boards, however, the structure in this sector could not be as simple. Special procedures were adopted so that a section of data could be set up for each GCE board. Each such section contained all those pupils taking at least one subject in the appropriate board, but no pupils not taking such an examination. It should be remembered that a pupil may enter GCE examinations in more than one GCE board as well as one CSE board. Hence different data sections could overlap by having pupils in common: the sections relating to different GCE boards could overlap with each other and with the CSE sections. Because of the lack of overlap between CSE sections it was possible to form three groupings of five, five and four CSE boards to enable some analyses to be carried out more conveniently. Larger groupings were not possible, because of machine restrictions.

The main analysis proceeded in a number of stages. The first stage was to investigate the age effect as described above. The next stage was to produce results for each CSE board for each of the selected subjects, separately for boys and girls and for boys plus girls except for housecraft (girls only), technical drawing and woodwork (boys only). Results were also produced for all pupils attempting at least one CSE examination in the given board. Because there was no overlap of candidates between CSE boards, the results for a given subject were then combined across all CSE boards to give results for the CSE sector. The combination process included suitably weighting the results of each board to give a true national picture.

Because of the overlap of candidates between GCE boards, a different strategy had to be adopted for the GCE sector. Results within boards were calculated in much the same way as results for individual CSE boards, except that entries for young candidates were used to substitute for early entries by candidates in the 16 + age group and, of course, it was necessary to weight results by CSE region to obtain the true national picture. The results for the GCE sector, as a whole, were obtained from the three large groups of data defined by CSE board as described above. Within each of these three sections, results were calculated for all GCE candidates in the specified subjects, or for all GCE candidates as appropriate. Results for the three sections were then combined to give results for the whole GCE sector.

The final stage was to obtain results for the whole examination sector in CSE and GCE combined. This was carried out in the same way as for the GCE sector totals, except that a pupil was included if he was entered for a specified subject at either CSE or GCE or both, instead of only for GCE.

The study was concerned with the level and range of ability of sub-groups of the 16+ age group and the size of each group. The size was calculated both as the actual number of pupils in the sample falling into the sub-group and as the weighted estimate, derived from the sample, of the number of pupils in the population falling into the sub-group. In addition, the mean and standard deviation of the Test 100 scores were estimated for the appropriate sub-group of the population, being measures of level and range of ability respectively. The distribution of Test 100 scores for each sub-group of the population was also estimated.

The way in which the design described above was put into operation is described in Chapter 3 with a report of the collection of data and subsequent preparation for the analyses. A technical description of the methods used to implement the aims and the design are given in Appendix B.

3 The data

Data collection

The design of the investigation required a sample of about 20 schools representative in type and sex of the schools in each CSE board region and these were selected from a list of all secondary schools with pupils in the 16+ age group supplied by the Department of Education and Science. The schools were grouped in Local Education Authority areas within CSE board regions and characterized by their type (modern, grammar, comprehensive, other secondary, direct grant and independent) and the sex of the school intake. The most up-to-date information available at the time of sampling was that of January 1973, the year prior to the study, so that it was necessary to draw the sample from those data. Information was subsequently available for January 1974 and a check was then made of the actual representativeness of the 1974 sample. The sample schools were selected by taking every nth school from a random starting point within the list of each CSE board region; (n being dictated by the proportion of the total number of schools in the region required to obtain 20 per region). Schools which had taken part in the 1973 Comparability Study (Willmott, 1977) had been assured that they would not be involved in 1974 and so such schools which had been drawn in the 1974 sample were replaced immediately. Since it was anticipated that the schools might find it difficult to undertake the formidable task being asked of them, two extra schools of the same type and sex intake as the sample schools were selected in advance to act, if required, as replacements for each sample school.

With the permission of the Chief Education Officers concerned, the sample schools were invited to take part in the investigation. As soon as a school notified its inability to participate the first replacement school was contacted and later the second if it was found to be necessary. The first contacts with all the schools were made in November 1973 but, in an attempt to obtain as good a sample as possible, approaches to replacement schools continued well into the Spring Term of 1974 when testing was taking place.

It was planned to give Test 100 to every pupil in the 16+ age group and to the 'young candidates' (i.e. early entries to GCE) in each sample school. Since it was of course necessary to ensure that the testing was carried out uniformly and under examination conditions, schools were likely to be presented with formidable organizational problems, particularly concerning timetabling and space. The most willing of schools might therefore find themselves unable to participate. Experience had shown that the period of the 'mock' examinations when school halls, etc. were prepared for examinations was favoured by many schools. In order to allow schools flexibility in fitting in the testing to suit themselves, schools were allowed to carry out the testing any time during the spring term. There is no doubt that this arrangement improved the chances of schools being able to take part.

It was agreed with staff of the Schools Council that the complicated administrative task presented to the schools should be simplified as much as possible and as a result schools were asked to test all fifth-year pupils, all pupils in the 16+ age group in the first-year sixth and all likely 'young candidates' for GCE O-level examinations. These categories were described in the instructions to schools as follows:

> The pupils to be tested are:
> 1 All 1973/74 fifth-year pupils (i.e. in the fifth year of secondary education after 11+, the year from which CSE and GCE O-level candidates are generally drawn). This includes those not entering for a public examination in the summer of 1974, those leaving at Easter as well as candidates for the CSE and GCE O-level examinations in the summer of 1974.
> 2 All 1973/74 sixth-year pupils born between 1 September 1957 and 31 August 1958 (i.e. those who will be 16 between 1 September 1973 and 31 August 1974).
> 3 All 1973/74 fourth-year pupils who are likely to be candidates for at least one GCE O-level examination in the summer of 1974 (i.e. those sitting an examination a year earlier than is usually the case nationally).

Thus, some pupils in the fifth form who were older than the 16+ age group ('over-age pupils') were included in the testing. Their answer sheets were removed later in the analysis of data. It was possible that a small number of the 16+ age group were in the second year of their A-level course. These were not included because demands on the schools in which this might occur were already great enough and it was estimated that the number would be very small indeed. While these were likely to be very able 16-year-olds indeed, at the other end of the ability range there were also likely to be some pupils who were very backward and in need of remedial teaching. It was anticipated that teachers might be reluctant to ask such pupils to take the test. In addition there were likely to be immigrant pupils whose understanding of English was insufficient to enable them to read Test 100 adequately. On the other hand, it was very important that as many as possible of the 16 + age group should be tested. It was left to the head of each school, therefore, to make a decision about each pupil whose understanding of English was very poor or who was considered to be in need of remedial teaching for other reasons ('remedials'). Schools were asked to test all pupils on their return to school who had been absent on the day of testing.

Since it was very important that all the 16 + age group should be accounted for, even if they were absent or considered to be 'remedial', schools were asked to complete a testing log giving details for the fourth, fifth, and sixth year separately, of the numbers of:

1 Pupils in each of the categories described above, that is, required for testing.
2 Pupils actually tested.
3 Remedial and immigrant pupils not tested on the head's instructions.
4 Long-term absentees not tested.

The figures given by each school were checked for discrepancies between the number given in No. 1 above and the total of those in 2, 3 and 4. The number of answer sheets actually recorded on the computer was later compared with the number given in No. 2 above with the 'over-age' candidates removed.

All those tested were required to mark their answers to Test 100 questions on a test answer sheet designed to be read optically by a document reading machine. Very specific instructions were given to pupils concerning the correct method for marking the answer sheets and in particular they were asked to ensure that the marks were made in the correct position for optical reading later.

Information concerning the examinations entered by all the 16 + age group in the summer of 1974 was generally given in the first instance by the schools, which were asked for the names of all boards with which they entered candidates. In 1973 and previous years information had been obtained only about the main board used by a school in the study. In 1974, for the first time, information on all boards used was obtained. Details of subjects (and grades for the comparability study) were later supplied by examining boards, and as explained in Chapter 2, details of examinations entered prior to summer 1974 were obtained from pupils themselves. The subjects and boards were allocated code numbers. The GCE boards were numbered 01–08 and the CSE boards 11–24. Examinations entered prior to 1974 were given a board code 00. The subject coding system will be described in the next section. Some 229 254 subject entries were coded and, together with Test 100 scores, optically read, selectively checked and analysed in approximately seven months. The data in the form of distribution of Test 100 scores were given to the Schools Council and the examination boards as background information for the report on the feasibility studies being carried out into the practicalities of introducing a single examination system at 16+. (Schools Council, 1975)

Subject classification

In the course of collecting information for the study of the 1974 summer examination 447 different syllabus titles were found, either as designations for the Mode I syllabuses published by the GCE and CSE examining boards or for schemes submitted by schools in the sample under the conditions of Mode II and Mode III. Although an investigation of the ability of candidates entered for different syllabuses within a subject area might have been an interesting exercise it was clearly financially impracticable, and some grouping of data obtained from candidates following different syllabuses was essential.

As described in Chapter 1 the study of the examinations in 1974 was designed to investigate two aspects of the public examination system: the comparability of grading standards in GCE O-level and CSE examinations and the ability of the 16+ age group, from which these examination candidates are generally drawn. The requirements of both aspects of the study had to be borne in mind in grouping data from entries under different syllabuses.

Two important and distinct requirements were, therefore, identified:

1 For the ability study, a record of every examination entered up to the age of 16+ by pupils in the sample was needed.
2 For the comparability aspect, continuity with subjects investigated in the 1968 and 1973 examinations was required. Since the smaller scale of studies of 1968 and 1973 included only the more commonly used syllabus titles, it was important that in the grouping of syllabus titles in the much wider investigation of the 1974 examinations the essential character of the subjects, as understood in the 1968 and 1973 comparability studies, should not be changed.

All the published GCE and CSE Mode I syllabuses were scanned and grouped according to their title and content prior to receipt of the grade results. Mode III titles were added from the results sheet supplied by the boards but, in this case—since information on content was not available—grouping was based solely on the title of the syllabus. Grouping on this basis was felt to be reasonable since it is incumbent upon the boards to ensure that the title of a syllabus accurately reflects its content and indeed this is a particularly important task for the CSE boards in the case of schools' submissions under Mode III.

However, it was apparent that some of the published Mode I syllabuses with different titles overlapped in content. This was particularly the case across the different boards, which apparently act independently in the designation of syllabuses, a practice which leads to a multiplicity of titles. In general, however, within each sector (GCE or CSE) all syllabuses with the same title were grouped together along with syllabuses with different titles but similar content. There were a few cases (Latin and classical studies in particular) in which syllabus titles were the same but content differed so markedly that these had to be allocated to the appropriate group for their content alone, regardless of their actual titles. In many cases the same titles occurred in both the GCE and CSE sectors and were grouped under the same subject name, although content often differed in emphasis markedly across the two sectors, as might be expected.

It has to be emphasized that it was not envisaged—and the resources were certainly not available—that strict criteria should be adopted for the grouping of syllabuses into subject classes. Very general guidelines were in fact used. There were many cases in which the information was not available, as for example in Mode III. Options were often available within a syllabus and the particular choice of an individual school was not necessarily recorded on the board's results sheets. Mathematics syllabuses, for example, often offered a wide choice of topics outside a basic common core. The CSE and GCE sectors differed markedly in their English syllabuses: the CSE boards generally offered a syllabus covering language and literature, but nevertheless left a wide choice within the syllabus to individual schools, while the GCE boards provided separate syllabuses for language and literature. There were, however, exceptions to this pattern in each sector, particularly in the entries under Mode III.

In the event, 59 main subject classes were identified and allotted a subject reference code number and name. Syllabuses with uncommon titles and for which information on content was not available, as in Mode III, were allocated to one of nine groups of miscellaneous subjects. However, a Mode III syllabus with the same title as a Mode I syllabus (e.g. English, biology, etc.) was allocated to the same subject class as the Mode I, since presumably the board was satisfied that the title was appropriate. In any case, few boards gave any indication of the mode of the examination on the results sheets and it was, therefore, impossible to make a distinction without overburdening the boards with a request for this kind of information. Sixty-eight subject code numbers were allotted in all and this subsequently allowed further groupings to be made as the two aspects of the study (comparability and ability) required.

Appendix C contains a complete list of all syllabus titles found in each board grouped under their subject reference code number and name. It should be noted, however, that the inclusion of a syllabus title in the list does not necessarily imply that candidates following that syllabus were part of the sample since, as explained earlier, the boards' Mode I syllabuses were classified before the coding of entries began. All entries under each of these 68 subject code numbers were included in the national and sector norms. For reason of cost the subject and board norms were confined to those subjects which were the focus of the feasibility studies for a single examination at 16+. This required some further combining of syllabuses and finally the 18 subjects with the largest number of entries were chosen. One of these, English, was also subdivided into English language and English literature providing data for 20 subjects in all and estimates of the proportion of the 16+ age group taking them. Table 3.1 gives details of the subjects considered in the present report and the reference code numbers of the groups of syllabuses which contributed to each subject. It should be noted that throughout the report the term 'subject' refers to a group or a combination of groups of associated syllabuses. The name of the subject is descriptive of the kind of syllabuses included in it and is usually that of the syllabus title most commonly used.

Table 3.1   Syllabuses included in the subject norms

Subject	Code number of associated syllabuses*	Subject	Code number of associated syllabuses*
Art	01, 61	Geography	23
Biology	42–46	History	25
Chemistry	47, 48	Housecraft	14–17, 63
Classical studies	4, 5, 7, 8	Mathematics	23, 30
Commerce	10	Music	39
English language	21	Physics	51, 52
English literature	22	Religious studies	40
English	20, 21, 22	Social studies	54
French	31	Technical drawing	58
German	32	Woodwork	59

*See Appendix C for syllabus titles

The sample of schools

A sample of 280 schools was drawn together with a replacement sample made up of two extra schools for each sample school. As a result 374 schools were approached and a sample of 269 schools was obtained, 96% of the planned sample of 280 schools. These were drawn from the population as it existed in January 1973, stratified by type of school and sex of intake, as explained earlier.

SCHOOL TYPE

Table 3.2 Distribution of school type in CSE board regions: population, January 1973 (percentages)

CSE Board	Type of school						Total	
	Sec Mod	Gram	Comp	Other	D.G.	Ind	N	Per cent
11	31·8	13·5	7·6	15·5	1·8	29·8	547	100·0
12	42·1	12·2	26·5	7·2	2·4	9·6	375	100·0
13	32·0	13·9	19·7	4·8	1·9	27·7	516	100·0
14	31·5	11·9	35·6	1·5	2·7	16·8	656	100·0
15	24·6	12·0	49·8	1·7	1·3	10·6	301	100·0
16	41·7	17·6	21·6	6·9	1·7	10·5	408	100·0
17	42·9	17·9	23·8	3·8	1·6	10·0	627	100·0
18	31·2	11·8	23·2	3·2	4·4	26·2	474	100·0
19	22·7	12·0	43·1	6·2	6·2	9·8	225	100·0
20	34·7	9·9	33·4	1·4	14·9	5·7	141	100·0
21	6·4	18·9	40·1	13·8	3·2	17·6	312	100·0
22	22·4	13·8	39·7	1·1	1·7	21·3	174	100·0
23	45·9	16·0	22·6	1·1	5·3	9·1	638	100·0
24	34·9	16·0	39·2	0·3	1·8	7·8	281	100·0
Total (N)	1915	817	1563	288	176	916	5675	100·0
Per cent	33·7	14·4	27·6	5·1	3·1	16·1	100·0	—
Actual 1974 (N)	1509	674	1976	217	176	906	5458	
Per cent	27·7	12·3	36·2	4·0	3·2	16·6	100·0	

The distribution of school type in the CSE board regions in England and Wales in January 1973, together with the overall distribution in January 1974 is given in Table 3.2. Three points emerge very clearly which have implications for the design and reporting of the study:

1 The total number of schools in each region ranged from 141 to 656. Weighting of the data was clearly necessary in estimating the statistics for the population from a sample of approximately the same number of schools in each region.
2 School type was unevenly distributed across the regions: for example, Board 20 had a much higher proportion of direct grant schools than the other boards; the proportion of independent schools ranged from 5·7 to 29·8%; similarly, comprehensive schools were unevenly spread across the regions. While an uneven distribution of school type within the maintained sector does not necessarily imply an uneven distribution of pupil ability across the regions, it may be argued, for example, that a higher proportion of direct grant schools in a particular region may influence the outcome of an attempt to measure pupil ability across the regions.

3 In January 1974 there were only 5458 schools compared with 5675 in the previous year, a decrease of 217 schools. This decrease was largely accounted for by the disappearance of 620 secondary modern, grammar and other secondary schools and the appearance of 413 comprehensive schools, in addition there were 10 fewer independent schools in 1974.

These changes were reflected in the sample: 20 of the schools identified by their DES numbers as secondary modern, grammar or other secondary schools in January 1973 were described as comprehensive in January 1974. It was not within the brief of the study to explore variations in ability in different types of schools and information on the effect of possible changes of type on the 16+ age group was not sought. However, if, for example, a sample grammar school became a comprehensive by amalgamating with a secondary modern the resulting comprehensive school was likely to have more pupils. As will be demonstrated later in this section, this had implications for the method of estimating the total number of pupils in the 16+ age group from the sample.

Table 3.3 gives the distribution of school type in the sample for each CSE board region, the numbers in each category are too small to describe

Table 3.3   Distribution of school type in CSE board regions: sample, January 1973

CSE Board	Type of School						Total
	Sec Mod	Gram	Comp	Other	D.G.	Ind	
11	6	3	2	3	—	6	20
12	7	3	4	1	1	2	18
13	6	3	4	—	1	6	20
14	6	2	7	1	—	4	20
15	5	2	10	—	1	1	19
16	9	2	4	1	—	1	17
17	8	2	6	1	—	2	19
18	6	2	6	1	1	6	22
19	5	2	9	2	1	1	20
20	7	1	7	—	3	—	18
21	4	4	7	3	—	3	21
22	5	3	7	—	—	3	18
23	9	4	3	—	—	2	18
24	7	3	7	—	—	2	19
Total	90	36	83	13	8	39*	269
Per cent	33·5	13·4	30·9	4·8	2·9	14·5	100·0

*All except two were recognized efficient by the DES

in terms of percentages and the representativeness of the sample was, therefore, checked over all regions combined and is shown in Table 3.4. With the exception of a very slight oversampling of comprehensive schools the sample seems to give an adequate representation of the population.

Table 3.4 Distribution of school type: population and sample, January 1973

School type	Number of schools		Per cent of schools	
	Population	Sample	Population	Sample
Sec Mod	1915	90	33·7	33·5
Grammar	817	36	14·4	13·4
Comp	1563	83	27·6	30·9
Other	288	13	5·1	4·8
Direct grant	176	8	3·1	2·9
Independent	916	39	16·1	14·5
Total	5675	269	100·0	100·0

Table 3.5 Distribution of boys, girls and mixed schools in CSE board regions: population, January 1973 (percentages)

CSE Board	Boys	Girls	Mixed	Total	
	Per cent	Per cent	Per cent	N	Per cent
11	26·9	33·3	39·8	547	100·0
12	10·7	11·2	78·1	375	100·0
13	21·9	24·6	53·5	516	100·0
14	16·6	18·1	65·3	656	100·0
15	10·3	12·6	77·1	301	100·0
16	17·4	17·9	64·7	408	100·0
17	19·1	19·0	61·9	627	100·0
18	21·1	19·2	59·7	474	100·0
19	20·0	20·9	59·1	225	100·0
20	17·0	22·7	60·3	141	100·0
21	30·4	36·9	32·7	312	100·0
22	21·3	25·9	52·8	174	100·0
23	21·6	22·7	55·7	638	100·0
24	7·5	8·2	84·3	281	100·0
Total (N)	1091	1198	3386	5675	100·0
Per cent	19·2	21·1	59·7	100·0	
Actual 1974 (N)	998	1099	3361	5458	
Per cent	18·3	20·1	61·6	100·0	

SEX OF SCHOOL INTAKE

In view of the known difference in response to Test 100 by boys and girls described in Chapter 1, it was important to ensure that the sample should adequately represent the sex of the school intake in the population. The distribution of boys, girls and mixed schools in the CSE board regions is given for the population in Table 3.5, for the sample in Table 3.6 and a comparison of the population and sample over all regions appears in Table 3.7.

Table 3.6　Distribution of boys, girls and mixed schools in CSE board regions: sample, January 1973 (numbers)

CSE board	Boys	Girls	Mixed	Total
11	4	6	10	20
12	1	2	15	18
13	6	7	7	20
14	2	3	15	20
15	2	1	16	19
16	2	3	12	17
17	3	1	15	19
18	2	8	12	22
19	3	3	14	20
20	2	2	14	18
21	8	8	5	21
22	5	4	9	18
23	4	5	9	18
24	1	2	16	19
Total	45	55	169	269
Per cent	16·7	20·4	62·9	100·0

Table 3.7　Distribution of boys, girls and mixed schools in CSE board regions: population and sample, January 1973

Sex of school intake	Number of schools		Per cent of schools	
	Population	Sample	Population	Sample
Boys	1091	45	19·2	16·7
Girls	1198	55	21·1	20·4
Mixed	3386	169	59·7	62·9
Total	5675	269	100·0	100·0

As in the case of school type there were considerable differences between the regions in the proportion of mixed schools. The sample appears to reflect satisfactorily the population in England and Wales overall in the case of girls' schools. Boys' schools however may be slightly under-represented and mixed schools over-represented.

THE SAMPLE SCHOOLS ENTRY TO GCE BOARDS

Information concerning all the GCE boards entered by pupils in the sample schools was obtained from the schools themselves. Table 3.8 shows the numbers of GCE and CSE boards entered by the sample schools and Table 3.9 the number of sample schools in each CSE board region which entered candidates for the examination of each GCE board. Schools entering with more than one GCE board appear in the table more than once. GCE boards 1, 2 and 7 are clearly very popular but, whereas board 7's clientele is spread fairly evenly over the country, boards 1 and 2 draw most of the entries from three regions each.

Table 3.8 Numbers of sample schools entered for various numbers of GCE and CSE boards

		Number of CSE boards entered		Total
		---	---	---
		0	1	
	0	0	20	20
	1	24	139	163
Number of GCE boards entered	2	6	62	68
	3	2	13	15
	4	0	3	3
	Total	32	237	269

The sample of pupils

From the figures entered on the testing log by each school, it was anticipated that 33 958 pupils should have been tested in the 269 schools. 610 of these were subsequently excluded because they were older than the 16+ age group, giving an expected total of 33 348 pupils in the sample. These included all the 16+ age group and the young candidates. These

Table 3.9   Number of schools within each CSE region entering candidates for each GCE board

CSE board region	Sample schools in each region	Entries for GCE	GCE board								Total for all boards
			1	2	3	4	5	6	7	8	
11	20	—	11	—	4	3	—	1	10	—	29
12	18	1	—	7	8	1	—	—	2	—	18
13	20	—	5	—	6	5	—	3	8	—	27
14	20	1	7	—	5	6	—	4	9	—	31
15	19	—	—	—	1	—	18	1	—	—	20
16	17	4	2	2	5	3	—	—	6	—	18
17	19	3	1	8	2	1	—	—	10	—	22
18	22	2	4	—	11	4	—	1	9	4	33
19	20	3	3	11	3	—	—	2	8	—	27
20	18	3	2	15	1	—	—	1	5	—	24
21	21	—	18	—	1	—	—	2	11	—	32
22	18	1	12	—	1	—	—	1	9	—	23
23	18	2	—	14	1	—	—	—	8	—	23
24	19	—	2	14	—	1	—	—	11	—	28
Total	269		67	71	49	24	18	16	106	4	355

figures were compared with the number of pupils recorded finally as having a test score, school by school. 33 089 pupils' actual test scores were recorded, 259 fewer than expected. Table 3.10 shows the number of pupils, with test scores in the 16+ age group and the 'young candidates', and compares them with the expected total number in each CSE region. (Table D.1 gives the actual number of pupils in the sample separately for the fourth-, fifth- and sixth-year groups.)

It is indeed remarkable that the discrepancy between the actual and expected numbers of pupils was so small and this indicates the care and perseverance with which the schools undertook the burdensome tasks required of them. The descrepancy was due either to some inaccuracy in the figures on the testing logs or to losses during the transfer of data to the computer. However, it was not possible to identify the categories to which the 259 'missing' pupils belong; they may indeed be in the 16+ age group, but on the other hand they may be 'over-age' or simply do not even exist and are the result of a clerical error by individual schools in completing the log. (Some examples of this were found.) However, for the purpose of estimating the population it was assumed that the 259 'lost' pupils were absent and were in the 16+ age group in the same proportion as those recorded as having a test score.

Of more concern was the relatively large number of pupils not tested because they were long-term absentees. 3670 were recorded by the

Table 3.10   The sample of pupils; actual and expected*

CSE board region	Number of pupils				Discrepancy between (a) and (b)
	Actual (a)			Expected (b)	
	16+	Young	Total	16+ and young	
11	1905	332	2237	2270	−33
12	2155	35	2190	2199	−9
13	2231	403	2634	2675	−41
14	2477	87	2564	2596	−32
15	2236	90	2326	2334	−8
16	2253	103	2356	2372	−16
17	2199	100	2299	2297	+2
18	2260	105	2365	2397	−32
19	2550	132	2682	2705	−23
20	2150	259	2409	2417	−8
21	2118	231	2349	2378	−29
22	1838	166	2004	2019	−15
23	1942	85	2027	2028	−1
24	2424	223	2647	2661	−14
Total	30738	2351	33089	33348	−259

*From figures supplied by schools

schools on their testing logs as being required for testing (i.e. in the categories described in the first section of this chapter) but were absent. A further 311 pupils were not tested because they were designated as 'remedial' by the head of the school. Table D.2 gives the number for each year group in each CSE board region. Their ages were not known and some of them may have been 'over-age' pupils in the 5th year. As a working basis it was assumed that they were in the 16+ age group in the same proportion as those with test scores in their particular year group.

Estimates of the 16+ age group population

The total number of pupils in the 16+ age group in the population was estimated by increasing the number of pupils in the sample in the ratio of the number of schools in the sample to the number in the population in each CSE board region separately (i.e. 1 in *n* as for sample). The total population in the 16+ age group in maintained, direct grant and independent schools was estimated to be 719 827 pupils. Table 3.11 gives the estimated total number of pupils in the 16+ age group for each CSE board region and the proportions estimated from the sample of the 16+ age group with test scores, the absentees (including the 'discrepancy')

Table 3.11   Estimate of the 16+ age group population in each CSE board region, 1974

CSE board region	Number of pupils in 16+ age group estimated from							
	Sample with test scores		Sample absentees		Sample remedials		Total	
	No.	%	No.	%	No.	%	No.	%
11	51 435	91·8	4361	7·8	232	0·4	56 028	100·0
12	45 255	94·1	2829	5·9	—	—	48 084	100·0
13	58 006	92·5	4029	6·4	703	1·1	62 738	100·0
14	81 741	88·1	10 792	11·6	260	0·3	92·793	100·0
15	35 776	81·9	7742	17·7	143	0·4	43 661	100·0
16	54 072	92·3	4367	7·5	143	0·2	58 582	100·0
17	72 567	90·0	7164	8·9	883	1·1	80 614	100·0
18	47 460	89·8	5206	9·8	224	0·4	52 890	100·0
19	28 050	89·1	3270	10·4	151	0·5	31 471	100·0
20	17 200	84·9	2752	13·6	316	1·5	20 268	100·0
21	29 652	75·2	8150	20·7	1639	4·1	39 441	100·0
22	16 542	86·1	2516	13·1	157	0·8	19 215	100·0
23	67 970	91·7	5648	7·6	517	0·7	74 135	100·0
24	36 360	91·1	3444	8·6	103	0·3	39 907	100·0
Total	642 086	89·2	72 270	10·0	5471	0·8	719 827	100·0

and remedial pupils. (Table D.3 gives the numbers in each school year group.) The overall proportion of the age group for whom no ability scores could be estimated—that is, the absentees★ and remedials—was 10·8% but there was considerable regional variation ranging from an overall proportion of absentees and remedials of 25% in Board 21 to 6% in Board 12. Its likely effect on the estimate of the ability of the 16+ age group as a whole and examination candidates in particular is discussed in Chapter 4.

The information derived from this study was required by the Schools Council in time to consider the reports on the feasibility of the single examination at 16+. Estimates of the 16+ age group population and examination candidates were based on the ratio of the sample to the population of schools from the only information available at the time, the DES data for January 1973. Since it was the proportion of the 16+ age group sitting public examinations and not the numbers which was of interest, the accuracy of the estimation of the actual number of pupils in the 16+ age group was not vital. However, information has subsequently become available which has allowed the accuracy of the estimates of

★Throughout the remainder of the report the absentees will include the 259 'lost' pupils 'discrepancy' described on pp 27–29.

numbers of the total population of the 16+ age group in 1974 to be checked. The number of pupils aged 15 on 1 September 1973 in schools with pupils aged 16 was supplied by the DES and thus the total number of pupils in 16+ age group in the population and sample could be counted. These are given in Table 3.12, together with the number in the sample schools taken from the same source and increased by the amount of the sampling ratio and the number estimated as described above. The differences between methods 1 and 2 in Table 3.12 suggests an inaccuracy in the sampling ratio, and the difference between methods 2 and 3 an inaccuracy in the representativeness of the population by the samples, in terms of the average number of the 16+ age group (i.e. schools in the sample were larger than the population as a whole). These points will be discussed separately below.

Table 3.12   Estimates of the 16+ age group population compared

Method of estimating	No. of pupils in 16+ age group
1 Total number of pupils aged 15 on 1.9.73 in all schools (DES list).	665 543
2 Number of pupils aged 15 on 1.9.73 in sample schools (DES list) increased in ratio of sample schools (January 1974) to population of schools (January 1973).	712 697
3 Number of pupils in 16+ age group estimated from sample with test scores and absentees etc. increased in same ratio as in **2** above.	719 827

THE SAMPLING RATIO

It will be recalled from Chapter 2 that the sampling ratio was based on the number of schools in the actual sample at the time of testing in 1974 in relation to the number of schools in the population in 1973, from which the sample was drawn. However, the number of schools had decreased by 217 between 1973 and 1974 (see Table 3.2). The number of 15-year-olds in schools on 1 September 1972 is not available since many would have left. However, it is possible to make an approximate comparison of the number of the 16+ age group who would have been in maintained schools if pupils had been obliged to stay in school until 16. (Figures for independent schools are not available.) Table 3.13 gives the number of pupils born in the appropriate years to supply the 16+ age groups in January 1973 and 1974 in maintained schools. It will be seen that there would have been more pupils in the 16+ age group in 1974 than 1973. There were, however, 217 fewer schools in 1974 than in the previous

Table 3.13   The 16+ age group in 1973 and 1974 in maintained schools*

Date of birth of pupils	Number
1 September 1957 to 31 August 1958 (aged 15 at 1.9.1972)	648 850
1 September 1958 to 31 August 1959 (aged 15 at 1.9.1973)	670 821

*Department of Education and Science (1974)

Table 3.14   The ratio of sample in January 1974 to population of schools in 1973 and 1974 and pupils in 1974 and difference in population estimate obtained

CSE board region	Ratio of sample in Jan 1974 to population		
	Schools in population 1973	Schools in population 1974	16+ pupils in population 1974
11	27	26·2	25·4
12	21	19·3	19·3
13	26	25·7	24·1
14	33	31·5	27·1
15	16	13·9	14·4
16	24	23·6	21·2
17	33	31·9	30·2
18	21	20·7	19·5
19	11	10·7	10·9
20	8	7·8	7·0
21	14	14·4	14·2
22	9	9·6	9·5
23	35	34·5	36·8
24	15	14·1	15·2
All regions	21	20·3	19·2

Estimates of no. of pupils in 16+ age group obtained.	719 827	696 772	666 120
Discrepancy with actual no. of pupils in 16+ age group i.e. 665 543*	+54 284	+31 229	+577

*Total in DES list of schools used for sampling

year. A sampling ratio derived from the number of sample schools in January 1974 relative to the number of schools in the population at January 1973 therefore produced an over-estimate of approximately 8% in the population of pupils in the 16+ age group.

The use of the ratio of the number of pupils in the 16+ age group in the sample compared with those in the population would have given a more accurate estimate. Data on the population were not, of course, available in this way. Table 3.14 gives the ratio, board by board, calculated by school in 1973 and school and pupils in 1974 and compares the population estimates arrived at by the various methods described above. It is clear that a more accurate estimate of the population would have been derived from using the ratio of pupils in the sample and population in 1974 if the figures had been available.

SIZE OF THE 16+ AGE GROUP IN SAMPLE AND
POPULATION SCHOOLS

An over-estimate of the number of pupils in the population of the 16+ age group could have arisen from the size of the 16+ age group in the sample schools compared with that in the schools in the population. Table 3.15 gives, for population and sample, the number of schools and pupils in the 16+ age group and the average size of the 16+ age group in each CSE board region. Over all regions the average size of the 16+ age group in the sample schools was larger than that in the population (129 pupils per school compared with 122 in the population). Table 3.16 summarizes these comparisons for the maintained schools and the direct grant and independent schools and it is clear that the difference is more marked in the direct grant and independent sector, where the average number of pupils is 43, compared with 31 in maintained schools.

While the inclusion of schools in the sample with larger than average number of the 16+ age group would increase the estimate of the population to some extent, the proportion of independent schools in the sample as a whole was small enough to have a limited effect. The main reason for the over-estimate of the population must lie in deriving the sampling ratio from the actual number of schools taking part in 1974 in relation to the number in the population in the previous year. There was, however, no alternative to this method at the time the information was required for the report on the feasibility studies of one examination at 16+. The results reported in Chapter 4 are largely concerned with proportions rather than numbers and the over-estimate of the population of the 16+ age group should not invalidate the findings of this study.

Thus the sample of schools drawn from the population of schools in England and Wales provided an estimate of the number of pupils in the

Table 3.15   Average size of school in population and sample—January 1974

CSE board region	Population			Sample		
	No. of pupils in 16+ age group	No. of schools	Average no. of pupils in 16+ age group per school	No. of pupils in 16+ age group	No. of schools	Average no. of pupils in 16+ age group per school
11	50 024	524	95·5	1973	20	98·7
12	43 680	347	125·9	2261	18	125·6
13	57 187	513	111·5	2374	20	118·7
14	77 059	630	122·3	2845	20	142·3
15	39 634	264	150·1	2755	19	145·0
16	50 051	402	124·5	2358	17	138·7
17	73 932	607	121·8	2452	19	129·1
18	48 373	455	106·3	2478	22	112·6
19	31 617	213	148·4	2901	20	145·1
20	17 359	141	123·1	2495	18	138·6
21	40 302	302	133·5	2843	21	135·4
22	20 689	172	120·3	2183	18	121·3
23	74 912	621	120·6	2034	18	113·0
24	40 724	267	152·5	2680	19	141·1
All schools	665 543*	5458	121·9	34 632	269	128·7

*No. of pupils aged 15 on 1 Sept 1973 taken from DES list of schools used for sampling

Table 3.16   16+ age group in maintained and direct grant/independent schools: population and sample January 1974*

School sector	Population			Sample		
	No. of pupils in 16+ age group	No. of schools	Average no. of pupils in 16+ age group per school	No. of pupils in 16+ age group	No. of schools	Average no. of pupils in 16+ age group per school
Maintained	632 392	4376	144·5	32 631	222	147·0
Direct grant/ independent	33 151	1082	30·6	2001	47	42·6
Total	665 543	5458	121·9	34 632	269	128·7

*From DES list of schools used for sampling

16+ age group and from this an estimate of the proportions entering certain examinations (as described in Chapter 1) was calculated. The results are described in Chapter 4.

Test 100

Investigation of the operation of Test 100 continued in 1974 with a test analysis based on a 1 in 20 sample of 1714 pupils drawn from the complete sample of the 16+ age group. The results are presented in Table 3.17 together with the equivalent results for 1968 and 1973 (taken from Appendix A for comparison).

Table 3.17   Analysis on the operation of Test 100

	1968	1973	1974
Sample size	690	856	1714
Mean test score	44·3	40·8	36·1
Standard deviation of test scores	13·3	14·6	15·9
KR20 reliability	0·92	0·93	0·94
Number of items	80	80	80
Number of items attempted by 80% of sample	71	64	Not available

The higher reliability, larger standard deviation of test scores and lower mean score in 1974 reflect the fact that the whole ability range was tested in 1974 while only examination candidates were tested in previous years.

Age effect on Test 100

As described in Chapter 2, Test 100 scores of 'young' candidates were to be used instead of the scores of pupils in the 16+ age group who had taken a subject prior to summer 1974. It was therefore necessary to investigate whether or not Test 100 scores increased with the age of a pupil. The result indicates that the effect is not very marked, being in the order of a score of an additional 3·3 points for each extra year of age. Even in the subjects most commonly entered early, such as English language, young candidates account for only about 7% of entries. In view of this and the high standard error of the estimated age correction, it was decided not to attempt to allow for the effect of age on Test 100 scores.

4 Results of the study

Introduction

There are broadly two sets of results arising from this study: estimates of the distributions of Test 100 scores for various populations of pupils in the 16+ age group (as defined in Chapter 1) and estimates of the numbers of pupils belonging to each of these populations.

For each population of interest the full distribution of Test 100 scores was estimated and these distributions, or norms, were subsequently sent to the GCE and CSE boards. However, due to lack of space, this report contains only summaries of these distributions. In particular only the mean and standard deviation of each test score distribution is presented here. Estimates of the numbers of pupils belonging to each population are also reported in the form of percentages of the whole 16+ age group.

The populations of interest fell into four broad groups:

1 Those in the 16+ age group with examination entries regardless of subject or board of entry.
2 Those in the 16+ age group with examination entries in particular subjects regardless of board of entry.
3 Those in the 16+ age group with subject entries in particular CSE boards.
4 Those in the 16+ age group with subject entries in particular GCE boards.

The presentation of the major results is arranged in four sections to correspond with the four broad groups listed above.

Thus the major results are arranged as follows:

1 Estimated means and standard deviations of Test 100 scores and estimated population sizes for the following populations:
(a) The whole 16+ age group in schools (other than special schools for the handicapped).
(b) Those in the 16+ age group who enter at least one public examination before the end of the school year in which they have their sixteenth birthday (N.B. This includes examinations taken by these pupils either in summer 1974 or previously).
(c) Those in the 16+ age group who enter at least one subject in the CSE before the end of the school year in which they have their sixteenth birthday.
(d) Those in the 16+ age group who enter at least one subject in the GCE

36

before the end of the school year in which they have their sixteenth birthday.

2 Estimated means and standard deviations of Test 100 scores and estimated population sizes for the following populations:

(a) For each major subject, those in the 16+ age group who enter the subject (in GCE, CSE or both) before the end of the school year in which they have their sixteenth birthday.

(b) For each major subject, those in the 16+ age group who enter the subject at CSE before the end of the school year in which they have their sixteenth birthday.

(c) For each major subject, those in the 16+ age group who enter the subject at GCE before the end of the school year in which they have their sixteenth birthday.

3 Estimated means and standard deviations of Test 100 scores and estimated population sizes for the following populations:

(a) For each CSE board, those in the 16+ age group who enter at least one subject with the board before the end of the school year in which they have their sixteenth birthday.

(b) For each CSE board, and each major subject offered by that board, those in the 16+ age group with an entry in that board-subject before the end of the school year in which they have their sixteenth birthday.

4 Estimated means and standard deviations of Test 100 scores and estimated population sizes for the following populations:

(a) For each GCE board, those in the 16+ age group who enter at least one subject with the board before the end of the school year in which they have their sixteenth birthday.

(b) For each GCE board, and each major subject offered by that board, those in the 16+ age group with an entry in that board-subject before the end of the school year in which they have their sixteenth birthday.

Each of the above results is given for each sex separately as well as for the total sample (i.e. boys and girls together).

As mentioned in Chapter 1, Test 100 takes a particular view of ability. It is not true that someone who scores higher than someone else on the test is more able in every sense of the word. On the other hand, there is a great deal of information available on the use of this test which shows that scores on the test correlate well with grade performance (e.g. Willmott 1976 and 1977). One comparison which may well be biased, due to the particular view of ability taken by the test, is that between the sexes. It was almost always found to be the case in this study that, whenever a particular population of interest was split into boys and girls, the boys had the higher mean Test 100 score. Insofar as the particular view of ability taken by this test is concerned it is almost certainly the case that the boys were more able than the girls but it is quite possible that the position would be reversed should a different aspect of ability be assessed.

In summary, the first group of results allow one to see what proportion of the 16+ age group had taken no public examination, at least one public examination, at least one CSE subject, at least one GCE subject, or at least one CSE *and* one GCE subject before the end of the school year in which they had their sixteenth birthday. In addition, the mean and standard deviation of Test 100 scores in each of these populations is estimated.

The second set of results permits comparison of the mean and standard deviation of Test 100 scores among CSE entrants to a particular subject with the mean and standard deviation of Test 100 scores amongst GCE entrants to the subject. They also show what proportions of the 16+ age group have no entry in a particular subject, at least one entry in the subject (in one or other sector), at least one CSE entry in the subject, at least one GCE entry in the subject, or at least one entry in CSE *and* one entry in GCE in the subject, before the end of the school year in which they have their sixteenth birthday. Comparisons can be made either across sectors in a particular subject or across subjects in a particular sector.

The CSE and GCE board results permit comparison of the mean and standard deviation of Test 100 scores among those pupils having at least one entry with a particular board with the mean and standard deviation of Test 100 scores among those pupils having at least one entry with another board and to make similar comparisons of the test scores of pupils entering a particular subject with a particular board with the test scores of pupils entering the same subject with another board. They also show what proportions of the 16+ age group have at least one entry with particular boards or in particular board-subjects before the end of the school year in which they have their sixteenth birthday.

Besides the major results mentioned above a certain amount of other information has been obtained from the hand analysis of a small sample of 608 candidates from five CSE board regions. In particular estimates of the average number of subjects taken per candidate in the summer 1974 examinations and of the number of different boards with which the average candidate was entered in these examinations are presented.

Finally, as a result of earlier studies by the Examinations and Tests Research Unit (Nuttall, 1970 and Willmott, 1976) a certain amount of comparable information is available from previous years since 1968. Where this is available it is presented together with the 1974 information so that comparisons can be made.

The national picture

Table 3.11, in Chapter 3, gives the estimate of the size of the whole 16+ age group that was obtained by weighting up the sample results by CSE region, and also shows the estimated numbers of remedials and absentees in the population. These results are reproduced below for easy reference.

Number of pupils in the 16+ age group estimated from those in the total sample of 719 827:

took Test 100	642 086
did not take Test 100 due to absence	72 270
present but did not take Test 100, because classified as remedial	5471

In order to estimate the proportions entered for at least one CSE, one GCE or one public examination it is necessary to make some assumptions about the likely examination entries of the remedials and absentees since information on entries was collected only for the testees.

It was thought reasonable to suppose that the remedials were not entered for any public examinations and that the 72 270 absentees would include a smaller proportion of examination entrants than was found among those in the 16+ age group who were in school at the time of testing. The actual assumptions made concerning the absentees were as follows:

	Not entered for CSE	Entered for CSE	Total
Not entered for GCE	18 068 25·0%	25 294 35·0%	43 362 60·0%
Entered for GCE	10 840 15·0%	18 068 25·0%	28 908 40·0%
Total	28 908 40·0%	43 362 60·0%	72 270 100·0%

With these assumptions Table 4.1 is obtained.

Table 4.1 Numbers and percentages of pupils in 16+ age group entered for GCE and CSE examinations—1974 population

	Not entered for CSE	Entered for CSE	All pupils
Not entered for GCE	98 681 13·7%	246 967 34·3%	345 648 48·0%
Entered for GCE	133 422 18·5%	240 757 33·5%	374 179 52·0%
All pupils	232 103 32·2%	487 724 67·8%	719 827 100·0%

One thing which emerges from Table 4.1 is that a massive 86% of school children take a public examination at some time before the end of the school year in which they have their sixteenth birthday. Also over two-thirds of all school children take at least one CSE, over a half take GCE, and about a third take examinations in both sectors at some time before the end of the school year in which they have their sixteenth birthday. Since the sexes of the absentees and remedials are not known it is not possible to produce the equivalent of Table 4.1 for boys and girls separately without making further assumptions. However, based on those pupils actually tested, the following is the estimated division between the sexes:

Table 4.2   Numbers and percentages of boys and girls in the 16+ age group entered in GCE and CSE—1974

		Not entered for CSE		Entered for CSE		All pupils	
Not entered for GCE	B	39 723	12·3%	110 932	34·2%	150 655	46·5%
	G	35 419	11·1%	110 741	34·8%	146 160	46·0%
	T	75 142	11·7%	221 673	35·5%	296 815	46·2%
Entered for GCE	B	67 034	20·7%	106 476	32·8%	173 510	53·5%
	G	55 548	17·5%	116 213	36·6%	171 761	54·0%
	T	122 582	19·1%	222 689	34·7%	342 271	53·8%
All pupils	B	106 757	32·9%	217 408	67·1%	324 165	100·0%
	G	90 967	28·6%	226 954	71·4%	317 921	100·0%
	T	197 924	30·8%	444 362	69·2%	642 086	100·0%

The numbers for boys and girls are clearly very much in line, but a larger proportion of boys than girls enters for GCE only, while a larger proportion of girls than boys enters for both GCE and CSE.

Willmott (1976) gives similar results to those in Table 4.1 for every year since 1968 and these are reproduced in Table 4.3. Since his results involved only examination candidates the estimates are expressed as percentages of the total examination entry in each year rather than as percentages of the whole age group. The 1974 estimates derived from the present study are adjusted accordingly for comparison and incorporated in the table. Willmott obtains his data from *DES Statistics of Education* Volume II. The results from the present study include 16-year-old pupils who had been young GCE candidates in 1973 but who were not entered for either CSE of GCE in 1974, while the DES figures for 1974 do not, but these are likely to be few in number. With these exceptions

Willmott's figures should be directly comparable with those obtained in the present study and this fact is reflected by the closeness of the agreement between the respective 1974 figures. The most significant trend in this table is the steady increase in the proportion of examination candidates who have an entry in CSE and the corresponding decrease in the proportion taking only GCE during the same period.

There has also been a steady increase in the overall numbers of pupils entering for public examinations. Most of this increase is accounted for by the increase in the numbers of pupils entering for CSE, but there has also been an increase in the overall number of GCE entrants.

Table 4.3 Proportions of examinations candidates in the years from 1968 to 1974 who enter in particular sectors

		Not taken CSE		Taken CSE		Total	
		No.	%	No.	%	No.	%
Not taken GCE	1968	0	0	81 414	24·3	81 414	24·3
	1969	0	0	95 863	26·1	95 863	26·1
	1970	0	0	103 830	27·1	103 830	27·1
	1971	0	0	105 510	27·2	105 510	27·2
	1972	0	0	114 362	27·4	114 362	27·4
	1973	0	0	118 248	26·9	118 248	26·9
	1974	0	0	246 028	39·1	246 028	39·1
Present study	1974	0	0	246 967	39·7	246 967	38·7
Taken GCE	1968	127 558	38·1	125 631	37·6	253 189	75·7
	1969	133 751	36·4	137 771	37·5	271 522	73·9
	1970	128 138	33·5	150 776	39·4	278 914	72·9
	1971	116 762	30·1	166 133	42·7	282 914	72·8
	1972	112 863	27·0	190 370	45·6	303 233	72·6
	1973	116 427	26·5	204 352	46·6	320 779	73·1
	1974	113 854	18·1	269 582	42·8	383 436	60·9
Present study	1974	133 422	21·5	240 757	38·8	374 179	60·3
Total	1968	127 558	38·1	207 045	61·9	334 603	100·0
	1969	133 751	36·4	233 634	63·6	367 385	100·0
	1970	128 138	33·5	254 606	66·5	382 744	100·0
	1971	116 762	30·1	271 643	69·9	388 405	100·0
	1972	112 863	27·0	304 732	73·0	417 595	100·0
	1973	116 427	26·5	322 600	73·5	439 027	100·0
	1974	113 854	18·1	515 610	81·9	629 464	100·0
Present study	1974	133 422	21·5	487 724	78·5	621 146	100·0

SMALL SAMPLE RESULTS

It was decided to obtain some additional information relating both to the number of boards with which the average candidate in 1974 was entered and to the number of subjects entered by the average candidate. Accordingly a random sample of 608 pupils was drawn from a section of the main data set and a hand analysis was made. These 608 pupils were drawn from approximately 90 schools which were all situated in one or other of the following five CSE board regions: South East, North, Southern, East Anglian, East Midland. Because of the restriction to just five regions it is not possible to say how typical the results are nationally but these regions do give a reasonable geographical spread. To begin with fourteen of the 608 pupils were identified as accelerated sixth-formers who had taken their first main public examinations in 1973 as early GCE entrants and so these were excluded from the sample leaving 594 pupils. Some of these 594 pupils may have been fourth-formers who were taking just one or two subjects, such as mathematics, English or French in 1974, with the intention of sitting their first main public examination in 1975. Unfortunately there was no simple and reliable way to exclude these and so it was assumed that the 594 pupils were all taking their first main public examination in summer 1974 and Table 4.4 related only to their entries for that examination.

Table 4.4   Number of pupils entering with different numbers of GCE and CSE boards at their first main public examination in summer 1974 (based on small sample)

		Number of CSE boards		
		0	1	Total
Number of GCE boards	0	53	180	233
	1	152	171	323
	2	14	21	35
	3	0	3	3
	Total	219	375	594

Table 4.4. shows that quite a large proportion (38 out of 594) of pupils enter with more than one GCE board and three people in the sample were found to enter examinations with as many as four different examining boards in summer 1974. It will be noted that these figures are broadly in line with those in Table 4.1, except that the small sample contained a larger proportion of candidates since it did not include any absentees or

remedials and no adjustment was made for this fact. 166 pupils (28%) took only GCE, 180 pupils (30%) took only CSE and 195 pupils (33%) took both CSE and GCE.

The data, for the 541 candidates in the small sample, further revealed that the number of subjects entered by the average candidate taking his first main public examination in summer 1974 was 6·79. A further breakdown of these figures is given in Table 4·5. Unfortunately similar results obtained

Table 4.5   Average numbers of subject entries per candidate by sector in 1974 (based on small sample)

		Not taken CSE		Taken CSE		Total	
Not taken GCE	No of candidates	0		180		180	
	GCE entries		0		0		0
	CSE entries		0		5·23		5·23
	Total entries		0		5·23		5·23
Taken GCE	No of candidates	166		195		361	
	GCE entries		6·56		4·16		5·27
	CSE entries		0		4·27		2·31
	Total entries		6·56		8·43		7·57
Total	No of candidates	166		375		541	
	GCE entries		6·56		2·17		3·51
	CSE entries		0		4·73		3·28
	Total entries		6·56		6·90		6·79

in previous years are not strictly comparable, since 1974 was the first year in which data on all subject entries were collected while in previous years only entries in the more popular subjects were counted as entries. In addition, where a school entered with more than one GCE board in these earlier years, only entries with one of these boards were considered. However, the results of 1968 and 1973 are presented in Table 4·6. Bearing in mind that the figures for the average numbers of subject entries in Table 4·6 are under-estimates, there certainly seems to have been no increase in the examination load on individual candidates between 1968 and 1974. However, in every year, those candidates entered for both CSE and GCE have on average a greater examination load than those confining their entries to a single sector. This may be a consequence of their entering twice for certain subjects, such as mathematics or English; once in each sector.

Table 4.6 Average numbers of subject entries per candidate by sector in 1968 and 1973*

		Not taken CSE		Taken CSE		Total	
		1968	1973	1968	1973	1968	1973
Not taken GCE	No of candidates	0	0	3585	5477	3585	5477
	GCE entries	0	0	0	0	0	0
	CSE entries	0	0	4·9	4·0	4·9	4·0
	Total entries	0	0	4·9	4·0	4·9	4·0
Taken GCE	No of candidates	4809	5025	4955	6266	9764	11 291
	GCE entries	6·7	5·4	3·9	3·0	5·3	4·1
	CSE entries	0	0	3·4	3·0	1·7	1·6
	Total entries	6·7	5·4	7·3	6·0	7·0	5·7
Total	No of candidates	4809	5025	8540	11 743	13 349	16 768
	GCE entries	6·7	5·4	2·3	1·6	3·9	2·8
	CSE entries	0	0	4·0	3·5	2·6	2·4
	Total entries	6·7	5·4	6·3	5·1	6·4	5·2

*Taken from Willmott 1976

TEST SCORES

The means and standard deviations of test scores for the whole 16+ age group and for those taking examinations in either or both sectors are given in Table 4.7. The results are given for each sex separately as well as for the total sample. The grouped score distributions (total sample only) for 'the whole 16+ age group', those taking 'at least one CSE', 'at least one GCE' and 'at least one public examination' are plotted in Figure 1. The curves are drawn with equal area beneath them for ease of comparison. Although there is a significant separation between each of the means (e.g. the average GCE candidate scores nearly 12 marks more on the test than the average CSE candidate) there is also a fairly large degree of overlap in the distributions.

It will be remembered that there were a number of absentees who did not take the test. If these were a random sample from the population then the results would not be altered. However, it is reasonable to suppose that some of the absentees will be long term absentees and that these will be of below average ability. In addition nearly 1% of the age group were classified as remedial and were also not tested. The net result is that the mean test score given for the whole 16+ age group in normal (i.e. excluding special) schools is probably a slight over-estimate.

Table 4.7   Means and standard deviations of Test 100 scores for those pupils in the 16+ age group with at least one entry in the CSE and/or GCE before the end of the school year in which they have their sixteenth birthday (boys, girls and total sample separately)

			Not entered for CSE	Entered for CSE	Total
Boys	Not entered for GCE	Mean S.D.	20·56 7·07	26·68 9·35	25·07 9·20
	Entered for GCE	Mean S.D.	55·39 15·34	40·87 14·11	46·48 16·22
	Total	Mean S.D.	42·44 21·19	33·63 13·87	36·53 17·15
Girls	Not entered for GCE	Mean S.D.	19·03 8·07	23·74 8·23	22·60 8·43
	Entered for GCE	Mean S.D.	50·36 14·73	35·79 12·84	40·50 15·11
	Total	Mean S.D.	38·16 19·78	29·91 12·40	32·27 15·35
Total sample	Not entered for GCE	Mean S.D.	19·60 7·82	25·09 9·35	23·70 9·30
	Entered for GCE	Mean S.D.	53·21 15·01	38·28 13·47	43·58 15·75
	Total	Mean S.D.	40·44 20·71	31·70 13·34	34·39 16·48

It can reasonably be assumed, however, that none of the remedials were examination candidates. Equally, unless those examination candidates who were tested differed in ability from those examination candidates who were absent on the day of testing, the estimated distributions of test scores for examination entrants would be unaffected by the fact that not everyone was tested. It is possible, however, that the mean test scores for candidates in either or both sectors are also slight over-estimates. However, it is difficult to see why any bias introduced should affect the different sectors differentially and so comparisons across sectors should be valid in any case.

It will be noted that the results for boys and girls separately show that, overall, the boys score more highly than the girls by 4 marks. In the GCE sector there is a slightly bigger difference between the sexes of about 6

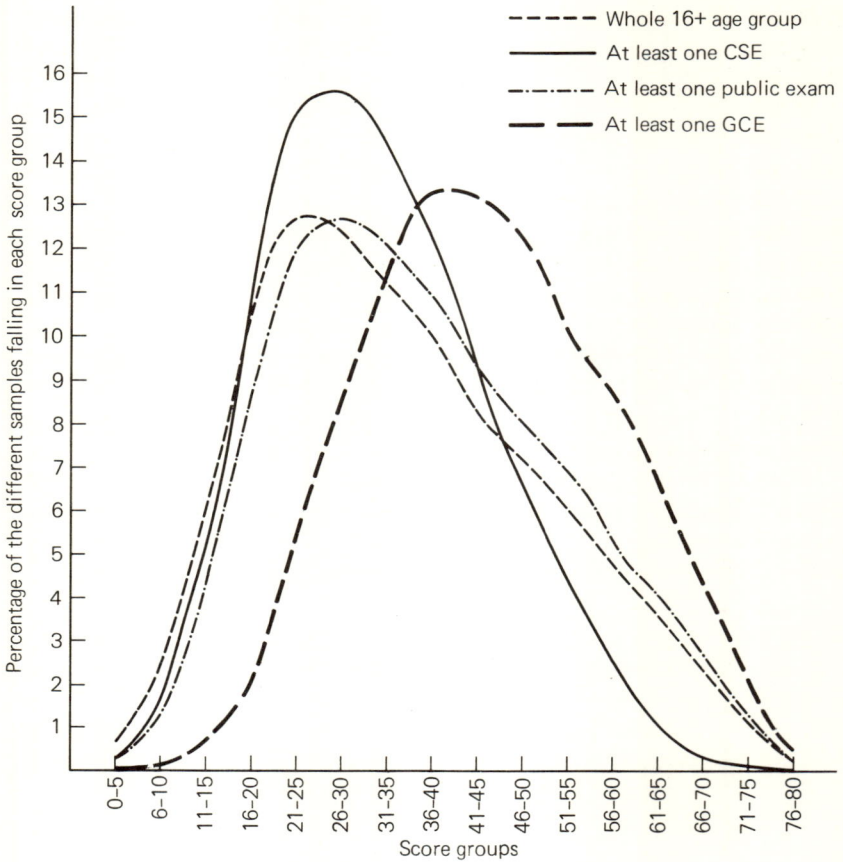

Fig. 1 Test 100 score distributions for examination candidates in the 16 + age group

marks while in the CSE sector the difference is only $3\frac{1}{2}$ marks. It is stressed that the test embodies a particular view of 'ability'. It is not claimed that the average boy is more able than the average girl, in every sense of the word. Also, the standard deviations of test scores for boys are uniformly greater than those for girls. Table 4.8 gives the means and standard deviations of test scores for those taking at least one CSE, one GCE and one public examination in 1968, 1973 and 1974. The results are given for 'total' sample only.

There appears to have been a clear decline in the average 'ability' and an increase in the spread of 'ability' amongst entrants to the public examination system between 1968 and 1974. Seen in conjunction with the increase in numbers of entrants over the same period it appears that there has been an influx of lower 'ability' candidates into the public examinations system.

It will be recalled that only the most popular subjects are included in 1968 and 1973 and these may tend to be the more academic subjects having the higher ability entries. However, the effect of this on the results of Table 4.8 should not be over-estimated. A candidate's score would be included in 1974, when it would not have been in earlier years, only if he entered none of the ten* or more most popular subjects which had been considered in earlier years. The number of people entering unusual subjects and only unusual subjects might be expected to be very small indeed and so their effect on the overall result would be minimal. Again it needs to be stressed that Test 100 embodies a particular view of 'ability'. It is only for those aspects of general ability measured by Test 100 that the above results are shown to obtain.

The influx of lower ability candidates into the examination system seems to have been gradually taking place even before the raising of the school leaving age, although clearly RoSLA itself must account for most of the very substantial change which took place between 1973 and 1974.

Table 4.8 Mean and standard deviation of Test 100 scores for sector entrants in 1968, 1973 and 1974

	1968		1973		1974	
	Mean	S.D.	Mean	S.D.	Mean	S.D
CSE candidates	39·0	11·7	35·9	12·3	31·7	13·3
CSE and/or GCE candidates	44·0	13·2	41·2	14·4	36·4	16·3
GCE candidates	48·0	11·7	46·9	12·5	43·6	15·8

The major subjects

This section begins with estimates of the proportions of the 16+ age group who enter for particular subjects, such as GCE mathematics, or CSE French, before the end of the school year in which they have their sixteenth birthday.

*In 1973 ten subjects were coded and in 1968 there were eighteen CSE and twenty GCE subjects coded.

It could reasonably be assumed that those pupils classified as remedial would not have any subject entries and so these could be included in the estimates. However, in order to include the absentees, it would have been necessary to make assumptions about the actual subjects for which they were entered. This was thought to be of debatable value, and accordingly it was decided to present results based only on those pupils who were actually tested (and whose examination entries were, therefore, collected) together with the remedials. This leads to an estimated population size of 647 557 rather than 719 827. Provided the pattern of entry amongst the absentees is much the same as among the remedials and testees, the actual proportions would be unaltered if the absentees were included.

Table 4.9 gives, for each of 20 major subjects, estimates of: the proportion of pupils who enter the subject at CSE before the end of the

Table 4.9   Pupils in the 16 + age group who take specified subjects in the CSE or the GCE sector before the end of the school year in which they have their sixteenth birthday (estimates in percentages)

Subject	Percentage of 16 + age group who enter for the subject at		
	CSE	GCE	Either CSE or GCE or both
Art	18·9	11·8	28·5
Biology	18·7	22·0	38·4
Chemistry	9·2	14·1	22·0
Classical studies	0·5	6·8	7·3
Commerce	4·6	0·9	5·3
English language*	5·5	44·0	48·9
English literature*	10·4	31·6	41·5
English	45·8	45·0	82·0
French	14·5	22·5	35·6
German	2·8	6·0	8·4
Geography	23·1	25·0	45·8
History	19·9	21·9	39·5
Housecraft	14·5	7·7	21·2
Mathematics	45·4	31·1	71·6
Music	1·8	2·2	4·0
Physics	14·4	16·0	28·5
Religious studies	6·1	9·1	15·0
Social studies	4·0	0·6	4·6
Technical drawing	12·2	4·7	15·0
Woodwork	7·1	2·2	8·7

*Defined so as to exclude CSE English whenever this comprises *both* language *and* literature

school year in which they have their sixteenth birthday; the proportion of pupils who enter the subject at GCE before the end of the school year in which they have their sixteenth birthday, and the proportion of pupils who enter the subject in one or other sector (or in both sectors) before the end of the school year in which they have their sixteenth birthday. (N.B. Readers will find full details of which board syllabuses are included under which of the 20 subject titles in Tables 3.1 and C.1.)

Perhaps the most interesting result to emerge from Table 4.9 is that 82% of pupils enter for some public examination in English before the end of the school year in which they have their sixteenth birthday and 71·6% do so in mathematics. Tables 4.10 and 4.11 give a further breakdown of these figures for English and mathematics respectively. Similar tables, for each of the other subjects, are given in Appendix E and Appendix F presents equivalent tables for boys and girls separately (on the assumption that there were equal numbers of each sex among the remedials).

Table 4.10   Pupils who enter English in GCE and/or CSE before the end of the school year in which they have their sixteenth birthday

	Not entered CSE	Entered CSE	Totals
Not entered GCE	116 696 18·0%	239 696 37·0%	356 392 55·0%
Entered GCE	234 217 36·2%	56 948 8·8%	291 165 45·0%
Totals	350 913 54·2%	296 644 45·8%	647 557 100·0%

Table 4.11   Pupils who enter mathematics in GCE and/or CSE before the end of the school year in which they have their sixteenth birthday

	Not entered CSE	Entered CSE	Totals
Not entered GCE	183 664 28·3%	262 669 40·6%	446 333 68·9%
Entered GCE	170 128 26·3%	31 765 4·8%	201 224 31·1%
Totals	353 792 54·6%	293 765 45·4%	647 557 100·0%

Tables 4.10 and 4.11 show that about 57 000 pupils take English in both CSE and GCE and around 32 000 do so in mathematics. Reference to the tables for boys and girls separately in Appendix F shows that a larger proportion of boys than girls takes mathematics in both sectors, while the reverse is true of English.

Because the definition of 'English language' adopted in this report specifically excluded CSE English, whenever this contained a component of both language and literature, it was decided also to produce an alternative table for English language in which entries for CSE English containing some component of language were specifically included. These results appear in Table 4.12, which shows that 81·6% of pupils take a public examination with an English language component before the end of the school year in which they have their sixteenth birthday.

Table 4.12 Pupils who take GCE and/or CSE with an English language component before the end of the school year in which they have their sixteenth birthday

	Not entered CSE	Entered CSE	Totals
Not entered GCE	118 724 18·3%	243 910 37·7%	362 634 56·0%
Entered GCE	237 378 36·7%	47 545 7·3%	284 923 44·0%
Totals	356 102 55·0%	291 455 45·0%	647 557 100·0%

TEST SCORES

Table 4.13 gives the means and standard deviations of Test 100 scores of those pupils in the 16+ age group who had entered for examinations in particular subjects in the GCE or CSE sector before the end of the school year in which they had their sixteenth birthday. In this case the results are necessarily based on those pupils actually tested. However, since remedials are unlikely to be examination candidates, it is unlikely that their exclusion will lead to bias in these results. Also, so long as those among the absentees who are candidates for a particular examination are not significantly more or less able than the candidates for this examination who were actually tested, again there will be no bias. In any case it is difficult to see why any bias should affect different subjects or sectors differentially and so comparisons across subjects or sectors should still be valid.

When comparisons are made within sex, within subject, across sectors, it can be seen that in every case the CSE entry is less able than the GCE entry and that in every case the group taking 'either CSE or GCE or both' lies between the CSE and the GCE groups in terms of ability. This is not surprising but it does give some assurance that Test 100 provides a sensible definition of 'ability', and one that conforms with our expectations. When comparisons are made within sex, within sector, across subjects, it can be seen that for total sample in CSE the high ability entries are in chemistry (mean score 38·0), French (38·3), German (40·9) and physics (36·3). For total sample in GCE the high ability entries are found in classics (57·7), French (52·7), German (54·4), mathematics (51·6), physics (54·5) and chemistry (55·7).

One thing that stands out in this table is the exceptionally high average ability of those girls taking physics in either sector. Since only a small proportion of girls actually studies physics, it appears that only the most able girls choose to study this subject. By contrast the entries in social studies for both sexes within each sector are well below average in terms of ability.

Similar results for the years 1968 and 1973 are reported by Willmott (1976), and these are presented in Table 4.14 together with the equivalent results for 1974. The results are for the total sample (i.e. boys and girls combined).

The trend is quite clear. In both sectors and in almost every subject there appears to have been an influx of lower ability candidates into the examination entry leading to a gradual drift downwards in mean test scores from 1968 to 1973 to 1974. This suggests that both the GCE and the CSE examiners are having to cope with candidates of lower average ability, in most examination subjects.

CSE board results

Table 4.15 gives the means and standard deviations of Test 100 scores for those pupils in the 16+ age group in each CSE board region. This gives a geographical breakdown of the national results for the whole 16+ age group, which were presented earlier. Clearly there are some fairly large differences among the mean scores for the total samples with regions 15, 16, 17, 19, 20 and 21 at one extreme, regions 11, 12 and 13 at the other, and regions 14, 18, 22, 23 and 24 in the centre. Nearly 9 points of test score separate region 11 from region 15. Another striking thing is the variation in the difference in mean test score between boys and girls from region to region. There is almost no difference between boys' and girls' mean scores within regions 11 and 15 and in region 21 the girls actually score higher than the boys on this test, supposedly biased in favour of boys. By contrast, the boys score higher by nearly 8 marks in region 13.

Table 4.13 Means and standard deviations of Test 100 scores for those pupils in the 16+ age group with entries in particular subjects before the end of the school year in which they had their sixteenth birthday (percentages)

Subject	Sex	CSE Mean	CSE S.D.	CSE and/or GCE Mean	CSE and/or GCE S.D.	GCE Mean	GCE S.D.
Art	B	29·25	11·30	33·93	14·01	43·35	13·63
	G	27·29	10·29	32·80	13·25	40·61	12·53
	T	28·27	10·85	33·34	13·62	41·77	13·07
Biology	B	34·81	11·11	45·86	14·31	51·88	11·76
	G	29·43	9·48	37·28	13·53	45·50	11·70
	T	30·93	10·25	40·36	14·41	48·18	12·14
Chemistry	B	39·14	11·52	49·91	14·06	56·91	10·74
	G	35·81	10·95	44·95	13·99	52·73	11·32
	T	37·95	11·43	48·31	14·23	55·66	11·09
Classical studies	B	38·89	11·81	58·93	11·34	59·96	10·30
	G	31·64	9·29	52·26	13·46	54·43	11·89
	T	34·53	10·96	56·12	12·71	57·70	11·31
Commerce	B	33·28	10·74	34·70	11·21	39·20	11·20
	G	28·74	9·15	28·53	9·60	36·15	10·02
	T	29·63	9·65	30·65	10·19	37·15	10·52
English language	B	32·74	11·13	47·94	13·94	50·01	12·91
	G	27·89	9·18	41·58	13·06	43·00	12·52
	T	30·54	10·57	44·72	13·87	46·41	13·18
English literature	B	35·06	11·56	47·47	14·13	51·71	12·15
	G	28·66	9·89	41·36	13·60	45·48	11·95
	T	31·61	11·16	44·15	14·17	48·34	12·43
English (20/21/22)	B	31·90	11·30	40·65	15·43	49·88	12·91
	G	27·34	9·53	35·22	13·95	42·88	12·53
	T	29·60	10·69	37·91	14·95	46·27	13·19
French	B	42·76	11·28	51·81	12·89	56·45	10·97
	G	35·40	9·95	43·38	12·90	49·22	11·38
	T	38·29	11·09	47·18	13·56	52·69	11·75
German	B	45·51	11·75	55·00	12·74	58·62	10·92
	G	37·97	10·61	46·96	12·58	51·27	10·97
	T	40·86	11·65	50·33	13·25	54·49	11·54
Geography	B	33·32	11·15	41·80	14·57	49·80	12·04
	G	30·13	9·92	38·75	13·53	45·33	11·64
	T	31·99	10·77	40·46	14·20	47·81	12·07

Subject	Sex	Sector					
		CSE		CSE and/or GCE		GCE	
		Mean	S.D.	Mean	S.D.	Mean	S.D.
History	B	32·47	10·81	41·64	14·74	48·77	12·52
	G	29·47	9·98	37·49	13·58	44·08	11·85
	T	30·96	10·51	39·55	14·32	46·46	12·42
Housecraft	G	27·55	9·58	31·72	11·71	39·75	10·93
Maths	B	33·57	11·06	42·03	15·18	53·36	12·06
	G	31·51	10·01	37·73	13·61	48·86	11·04
	T	32·54	10·60	40·00	14·62	51·57	11·87
Music	B	33·76	11·07	43·31	14·99	51·36	11·66
	G	31·21	10·27	39·57	13·50	46·37	11·61
	T	32·20	10·66	40·96	14·18	48·32	11·88
Physics	B	35·97	11·23	45·38	14·94	54·69	11·42
	G	38·04	10·97	48·02	13·65	54·00	11·00
	T	36·28	11·22	45·86	14·75	54·54	11·34
Religious studies	B	33·05	14·28	43·27	16·01	50·25	13·00
	G	28·69	10·16	37·04	13·15	42·54	11·88
	T	30·19	11·92	39·16	14·49	45·14	12·79
Social studies	B	24·79	9·97	26·66	11·01	39·94	9·55
	G	23·82	9·08	25·92	10·41	37·51	9·73
	T	24·27	9·51	26·26	10·70	38·45	9·73
Technical drawing	B	33·64	11·22	36·23	12·48	45·02	11·57
Woodwork	B	30·49	11·04	33·25	12·74	43·75	12·39

The comparison of the standard deviations for boys and girls in Table 4.15 reveals that in every region except region 21 there is a greater spread of ability among boys than among girls. This is in line with the prediction of Alice Heim (1970).

When the samples by region are restricted to those pupils making at least one entry at CSE then the results in Table 4.16 are obtained. This time the mean test scores from board to board are remarkably similar, which suggests that much the same criteria may be being applied in each region to determine which pupils should enter for CSE, even though the 'pools of ability' in each region appear to differ somewhat.

Another interesting facet of the comparison of Tables 4.15 and 4.16 is that, for every CSE board region except one, the mean ability of CSE entrants in the region is less then the mean ability of pupils in the region.

Table 4.14   Estimated mean test scores by subject entry—1968, 1973 and 1974

Subject	GCE			CSE		
	1968	1973	1974	1968	1973	1974
Art	46·0	43·5	41·8	35·6	31·8	28·3
Biology	50·9	50·2	48·2	37·2	34·7	30·9
Chemistry	56·0	55·2	55·7	42·4	41·0	38·0
English language	48·7	47·8	46·3	36·1	32·0	29·2
French	53·1	52·8	52·7	43·9	41·0	38·3
Geography	51·0	49·9	47·8	37·4	34·2	32·0
German	55·3	*	54·5	47·9	*	40·9
History	51·1	49·2	46·5	36·7	34·5	31·0
Mathematics	52·0	51·5	51·6	39·0	35·6	32·5
Physics	55·7	53·8	54·5	40·8	38·9	36·3
Religious education	46·3	*	45·1	34·8	*	30·2
Technical drawing	47·2	46·3	45·0	38·4	35·2	33·6

*Information not available

It could be informative to consider the equivalent figures from 1968 and 1973 in order to detect any influx of particularly high or particularly low ability candidates as entrants to CSE in any one region. Unfortunately the only available figures from previous years are based on entries rather than individual candidates. In other words, a candidate's test score is counted separately for each CSE subject which he enters. As there is a relationship between the number of CSE examinations a person takes and his ability (Willmott, 1975), this can lead to a substantial bias and so it was thought best to avoid such comparisons.

The tables given in Appendix G and Appendix H complete the results relating to individual CSE boards in 1974. These tables contain respectively the estimated numbers of candidates entered for particular

Table 4.15 Sample sizes and means and standard deviations of Test 100 scores for the whole 16 + age group by CSE board region (1974)

Board region	Boys			Girls			Total sample		
	n	Mean	S.D.	*n*	Mean	S.D.	*n*	Mean	S.D.
11	907	40·20	17·08	998	39·71	15·49	1905	39·94	16·26
12	1065	39·70	16·60	1090	34·36	15·27	2155	37·13	16·14
13	1138	42·42	16·55	1093	34·54	14·62	2231	38·56	16·12
14	1180	37·64	16·35	1297	33·80	14·13	2477	35·63	15·34
15	1313	31·85	14·87	923	30·19	14·05	2236	31·17	14·56
16	1138	34·05	15·35	1115	29·57	13·31	2253	31·83	14·55
17	1244	33·41	15·42	955	30·86	13·82	2199	32·31	14·80
18	956	38·25	15·54	1304	32·99	14·96	2260	35·22	15·43
19	1274	33·79	15·80	1276	28·68	11·88	2550	31·23	14·21
20	1265	36·40	19·32	885	27·79	12·51	2150	32·85	17·38
21	1046	31·01	15·69	1072	32·61	16·39	2118	31·82	16·06
22	1113	36·34	15·26	725	33·82	14·50	1838	35·34	15·01
23	931	39·10	17·91	1011	30·84	13·38	1942	34·80	16·24
24	1197	36·93	15·94	1277	31·46	13·68	2424	34·16	15·09
All*	324 165	36·53	17·15	317 921	32·27	15·35	642 086	34·39	16·48

*Estimates derived from weighting up the sample data by board region

Table 4.16 Means and standard deviations of Test 100 scores for CSE entrants by board (1974)

Board region	Boys		Girls		Total sample	
	Mean	S.D.	Mean	S.D.	Mean	S.D.
11	35.63	12·67	32·90	10·96	34·28	11·93
12	34·94	12·39	31·18	11·96	33·07	12·32
13	36·73	13·41	31·97	12·12	34·21	12·96
14	34·63	13·49	31·15	11·24	32·77	12·46
15	31·66	11·36	28·77	10·17	30·45	10·97
16	33·92	12·60	29·13	10·62	31·52	11·89
17	33·03	12·15	29·82	10·85	31·56	11·68
18	36·11	12·93	30·99	12·24	33·09	12·77
19	33·45	13·84	29·44	10·54	31·37	12·39
20	30·00	12·30	26·67	9·91	28·50	11·40
21	27·70	13·07	25·81	10·67	26·81	12·05
22	33·87	13·42	30·95	11·99	32·70	12·94
23	33·83	13·08	29·47	11·46	31·26	12·34
24	35·30	14·17	31·27	12·29	33·21	13·38
All	33·63	13·87	29·91	12·40	31·70	13·34

subjects with particular CSE boards and the means and standard deviations of Test 100 scores for these entrants.

Similar results to those in Appendix H for the years 1968 and 1973 appear in Appendices I and J respectively, although only a limited range of subjects were available for these earlier years. This information is taken from Willmott (1977).

GCE board results

The means and standard deviations of Test 100 scores for all candidates having at least one entry with particular GCE boards are given in Table 4.17. These show rather more variation than was found among the CSE board entries with Board 6 having a particularly able entry and Boards 5 and 7 at the other extreme. (Very few candidates for Board 8 were found in the sample; this reflects the fact that this is by far the smallest board in terms of numbers of candidates but also means that the mean scores shown are less reliable than those for the larger GCE boards.) There is a difference of over 12 points of score between the average candidates for GCE Boards 5 or 7 and the average candidate for GCE Board 6. Again there is some large variation in the differences between boys and girls scores from the same board entry, ranging from less than 2 marks difference in Board 1 to over 11 marks difference in Board 6.

As with the CSE board entry norms it is not possible to report suitable information from earlier years to enable the detection of trends, as the

Table 4.17 Means and standard deviations of Test 100 scores for GCE entrants by board in 1974

Board	Boys		Girls		Total	
	Mean	S.D.	Mean	S.D.	Mean	S.D.
01	46·35	14·10	44·66	13·04	45·46	13·58
02	49·44	13·55	40·56	12·58	45·30	13·83
03	48·87	12·58	43·79	12·08	46·02	12·56
04	48·31	13·46	43·91	13·03	45·76	13·39
05	42·58	13·04	35·96	11·23	39·80	12·74
06	55·19	11·40	43·82	13·56	53·16	12·59
07	42·79	12·10	37·52	11·02	40·38	11·92
08	42·84*	7·92*	38·25	11·40	38·78	11·15
All	46·48	16·22	40·50	15·11	43·58	15·75

*Estimate based on total sample of only 19 pupils

only previous results are based on entries rather than candidates and this would be liable to introduce a substantial bias into the comparisons.

The tables in Appendices K and L show, respectively, the estimated numbers of candidates entered for particular subjects with particular GCE boards and the means and standard deviations of Test 100 scores for these entrants while Appendix M gives similar results to those in Appendix L for a limited range of subjects in 1973. Again the source of this information is Willmott (1977).

5 Summary and discussion

The previous chapters have described a study which took place in 1974 and focused primarily on all pupils having their sixteenth birthday (the 16+ age group) in the school year 1973/4. This group of pupils was, for the first time, legally bound to remain in school at least until Easter 1974—and many until the summer—and thus 1974 provided the first opportunity of investigating the ability of the age group from which examination candidates are usually drawn. The aims of the study were to investigate the range and level of 'ability' of the 16+ age group and candidates entering CSE and GCE O-level examinations together with the proportion of the 16+ age group entering particular examinations. This information was also to be used for the evaluation of the common examination feasibility studies taking place at the same time. 'Ability' was defined for the purpose of this exercise as 'general' ability and, in operational terms, as scores on a test of general scholastic ability. Test 100 had been used in a number of previous studies into the comparability of grading standards in the CSE and GCE O-level examinations and had shown itself as a reliable test with a sufficiently close relationship to performance in the examinations to merit its use in the study reported here.

Test 100 was, therefore, given to a sample of pupils in the 16+ age group and scores derived from the exercise were used to provide an estimation of the 'ability' of the whole 16+ age group. An estimated 10% of the age group were long-term absentees who were not in school over a period of several weeks in which the schools were waiting to test them. The effect on the results of this study cannot be precisely defined, but assumptions were made, and it is anticipated that the estimates obtained are not unduly biased. Discovery of such a large proportion of absentees in the 16+ age group is not, of course, confined to this investigation. Statistics published by some of the examining boards show an increase in 1974 in the number of absentees from their examinations and, no doubt, reflect the fact that the increased number of examination entries include unwilling school attenders.

Information derived from the study was given to the Schools Council and all the examining boards in the form of norms (i.e. distributions of Test 100 scores) by sex, together with associated means and standard deviations for the whole 16+ age group, all examination candidates and certain sub-groups of candidates; these norms were produced for a number of major subjects.

The norms are summarized in this report in the form of means and standard deviations of Test 100 scores. In addition the proportions of the 16+ age group entering any public examination and particular subject examinations were estimated.

The study called for generous co-operation on the part of the 269 schools and involved over 33 000 pupils and an extensive research design to handle the large amount of data collected. This provided a wealth of facts and figures about candidates entering different public examinations in relation to each other and to the whole 16+ age group, and a summary of the results are to be found in the tables included in this report. Some highlights of these results are briefly discussed below.

Compared with 1973, in 1974 there was a large increase in the number of examination candidates, mostly in the CSE sector (53%), although there was also an increase in the overall number of GCE candidates (5%). This increase can, of course, be accounted for by the increase in the number of pupils remaining in school for the year in which examinations are usually taken as a result of raising the school leaving age. The ability of these new candidates was generally lower than the ability of candidates in 1968 and 1973. It was interesting to note that the average CSE candidate was of lower ability than the average pupil in the 16+ age group in 1974. 86% of the age group entered at least one public examination (82% took English and 72% mathematics). The 86% of the age group may be compared with the 60% of the age group for which the CSE and GCE O-level examinations were originally designed, although it was also accepted that the range of 'general' ability within a single subject would extend beyond the group for which the CSE examinations, as a whole, were designed. (See the first section of Chapter 1.) This expectation was fulfilled in the 1974 examinations.

Some overlap in the general ability range of CSE and GCE O-level candidates was anticipated also, but it is clear from the results of the study that the 'overlap' ability range is considerably wider than was expected. Just over 33% of the 16+ age group entered at least one CSE and one GCE O-level examination in 1974, compared with 34% taking CSE examinations only and 19% taking only GCE examinations. The introduction of O-level grades in the summer of 1975 may, however, affect the pattern of entry. The practice of entering for subjects in both sectors and the same subject in both sectors (double entry) should, of course, disappear under a common system of examinations. The introduction of a common timetable will certainly lead to the disappearance of double entry. There were considerable differences in the general ability (as measured by Test 100) of pupils in the 16+ age group across the CSE board regions, the mean scores ranging from scores of 31 to nearly 40. Large variation was also detected in ability of the entry, subject by subject in both sectors, with high ability entries in GCE classics, French, mathematics, physics and chemistry and, within the CSE sector, in chemistry, French, German and physics. In contrast, candidates in social studies were below average.

It was estimated that roughly 10% of GCE candidates entered examinations in more than one GCE board. This may be, in part, a reflection of the variety of syllabuses which are offered by the various boards. Some 447 different syllabus titles were classified in the course of the data preparation into 68 'subjects' which were further combined to give data for the subjects under scrutiny in the common examination feasibility studies. The extent to which syllabuses had to be combined to reflect the subject content of the common examination feasibility studies is indeed an indication of the width of the syllabus content which a single subject in a common examinations system would need to embrace. While such a diversity of syllabus content and titles provided by the examining boards may offer a wide choice to teachers, it provides a confusing picture to users of examination results. Many of the Mode III syllabuses are often designed with relevance to the vocational aspirations of pupils in mind and embrace subjects outside the traditional curriculum. The growing use of Mode III increases the likelihood of a proliferation of syllabus titles. In attempting to classify syllabuses it was found that those with the same title often differed considerably in content, while those with similar content had different titles. The time may soon arrive when some rationalization will become necessary if success or failure in a subject is to have some definitive meaning to users in terms of subject knowledge on the part of the candidates.

It is clear from this investigation of the 16+ age group in 1974 that a large proportion of pupils in this group were involved in examinations; only 14% were not entered for an examination. A survey carried out in 1966 of young school leavers (Schools Council, 1968) found that pupils and parents were anxious that education should provide vocational skills, and that courses should have relevance for pupils' future work. Teachers, on the other hand, while wishing to make the curriculum more relevant by bringing in new subjects or topics, saw this as a means of enriching the lives of pupils by developing aesthetic awareness and establishing a base for leisure-time activities. The titles of the syllabuses in Appendix C, particularly some of those under subject reference code numbers 60–68, indicate the kind of course being introduced under Mode III. These courses appear to be largely 'practical' courses and were no doubt designed to interest the RoSLA pupils. The increase in examination entries could also be interpreted as recognition on the part of teachers of pupils' and parents' aspirations, and the desire of pupils to leave school with some recognized qualifications.

It seems clear from the results of the investigation described in the report that the existence of both the CSE and GCE O-level examination systems, while offering a wide variety of syllabuses to suit a wide range of ability, serves also to increase the burden of examinations, particularly on pupils in the middle range of ability for whom the choice between entering CSE or GCE O-level examinations is difficult to make. In the event some enter the same subject in both sectors; others enter in one sector only. The large proportion of dual entries and the use of more than one GCE board suggests that many schools choose the syllabuses purposefully, to suit particular needs. The choice must in the end be with the teachers who have to take account of the needs of all their pupils. The constraints of the timetable and staffing may have to be weighed against the interests of individual pupils. A common examination would eliminate this problem and would appear to make the task of teachers easier. However, the difficulties of devising course syllabuses to suit such a wide range of ability as would appear to be necessary from the results of this study are all too evident.

In general the burden of examinations on pupils in the 16+ age group appears to be heavy. 86% of pupils in the group were taking at least one public examination and it was estimated that the 33% of pupils in the 16+ age group who were taking examinations in both sectors had on average 8·4 subject entries each; this should be compared with the 6·6 subjects each taken by the 19% taking GCE subjects only and the 5·2 subjects each taken by the 34% taking CSE subjects only. It is clear that, for those in the middle of the ability range of examination candidates, the burden of examinations must be particularly hard as they enter in both sectors. The larger average number of subjects taken by pupils entering in both sectors than those entering in one sector only illustrates the dilemma in which pupils in the middle range of ability find themselves—a dilemma which a common examination at 16+ would resolve. If the aim of those concerned with the well-being of young people is to 'educate them for life', then the burden and multiplicity of examinations for those in the middle of the ability range must be disheartening, since it can leave very little time to study for anything other than examination success. In this context, a common examination at 16+ would appear to be very desirable. Those who cling firmly to the established pattern of two systems of examinations at 16+ should take particular note of the fact that the dividing line between GCE and CSE candidates is not clear cut.

The report on the common examination feasibility studies made it abundantly clear that there were many difficulties in the way of a common examination which the feasibility studies were unable to resolve. The information in the present report suggests that there is an urgent need to make a further attempt to resolve these problems, so that a common examination system could be introduced. The present evidence suggests that this would alleviate the burden of examinations on a large number of examination candidates and allow time in the curriculum for those aspects of education which are not geared to examination success.

Appendices

Appendix A   Test 100: an excerpt from 'An analysis of GCE and CSE examination grades' by A. S. Willmott

EARLY MONITORING TESTS

For the first CSE monitoring experiment on the grade results of the nine boards in existence in 1965, a special test was commissioned. In 1964 the Secondary School Examinations Council approached the School of Education of Manchester University with a request to prepare 'a new multiple-choice test of "general scholastic abilities", suitable for experimental use in monitoring the CSE examinations' . . . The test was to have items calling for 'quantitative reasoning, data interpretation, synonyms, antonyms and other items designed to test general reasoning ability'. The test was composed of 100 items and it was found in the event that the items discriminated satisfactorily between the candidates within both the CSE and GCE samples chosen. Specimen items from this test are given in the 1965 monitoring report (Schools Council, 1966). Unfortunately, however, the test proved to be rather hard and the mean scores were about 55 in the GCE sector and about 30 in the CSE sector. Further, as the candidates were required to write out their answers to some questions—which then had to be marked by hand—the use of this test was far from ideal in terms of practicality. So a new test was considered for the 1966 exercise.

Test CP66, which was used in the 1966 and 1967 exercises, was the result of extensive discussions within an 'ad hoc test development committee which included teacher-examiners and staff of CSE examination boards as well as representatives of the Schools Council staff', (Skurnik and Hall, 1969). A test blueprint was laid down, spelling out the types of thinking on which it was agreed to base the test and indicating the content and types of items which might elicit responses from pupils using these types of thinking. Full details of the procedures are given by Skurnik and Hall (1969), but CP66 was a 90-item test of multiple-choice items, half of which measured linguistic aptitude or verbal ability and half of which measured quantitative thinking or mathematical ability. The items varied in style and were aimed at assessing 'both simple and complex association skills (or convergent thinking); power of interpretation or skill of evaluation of the quality and meaning of data or information given; and flexibility of thinking or the power to employ new patterns of thought and action'.

In the event, CP66 turned out to be a much better test than that used in 1965, with high reliability and discrimination, although rather speeded: in the CSE sector for example, the internal consistency reliability estimate was 0·96, although only 91% of the candidates attempted three-quarters of the items. This latter fact was not held by Skurnik and Hall to be too important as speed 'undoubtedly constitutes a small component of the criterion' (i.e. the examination grades being analysed). In terms of the correlation with subject grades, values of 0·3 to 0·4 were obtained, which the authors of the 1966 report indicate are 'not very high'. They then go on to point out that the general relationship between what is a 'searching measure of school attainment' and the reference test is higher than it might appear:

Correlations have been quoted separately for two populations (CSE and GCE) of highly restricted range and this, statistically, leads inevitably to diminished correlations . . . a short test of *attainment* would not be expected, in general, to correlate much higher than 0·7 with the corresponding subject grades and, in this light, the mean correlations of the reference test (a short *general abilities* test) with mathematics and English grades come out very favourably in both the CSE sector (0·44 to 0·52) and the GCE sector (0·42 to 0·49).

Test CP66 was used again in the 1967 monitoring work but, by the time the 1968 exercise was administered, the heavy use of this test and its slightly speeded nature led to the development of a new test, Test 100.

TEST 100

The blueprint of the test was similar to that used for CP66, since the aim was to construct a test very similar to CP66, but some consideration was given to the variety of aptitudes embraced by the Guilford model (Guilford, 1967). Many draft pre-tested items produced for but not used in CP66, plus 250 new items drafted by members of the (ETRU), were edited by the staff of the Foundation. The majority of items surviving this expert scrutiny were assembled into four draft tests, each of which was pre-tested in at least two schools. On the basis of the quantitative and qualitative evidence of the trials, a single revised test containing the best items was assembled according to the blueprint specification and was again tried in the field; this became the final test after one or two weak items had been replaced.

Test 100 is composed of 80 multiple-choice questions, mostly of the five-choice type. As in CP66, exactly half the items are designed to measure verbal ability and the other half quantitative ability. The items are arranged in order of increasing difficulty and in blocks of four or five items of a similar style and content. Five practice examples are provided to illustrate the different types of item and the method of recording answers. The time limit for the test proper is 50 minutes, the same as CP66. Since Test 100 has 80 items instead of the 90 in CP66, it was hoped that Test 100 would be less speeded.

(Nuttall, 1971)

In 1973, as in 1968, a 1 in 20 random sample of all candidates tested was taken in order to perform item and test analyses. Table A.1 gives the test analyses for these years.

In 1968, Test 100 performed well, with nearly 90% of the items being

Table A.1   Test analysis for Test 100—1968 and 1973

	1968*	1973
Sample size	690	856
Mean Score	44.3	40.8
(Mean score as a per cent)	(55.4)	(51.0)
Standard deviation	13.3	14.6
(Standard deviation as a per cent)	(16.6)	(18.3)
Reliability – KR20	0.92	0.93
Standard error of measurement	3.8	3.9
(S.E.M. as a per cent)	(4.8)	(4.8)
Number of items attempted by 80% of sample (as a per cent)	(88.8)	(80.0)

*Taken from Nuttall, 1971

attempted by 80% of the sample; the mean score is just over the mid-point of the range and the standard deviation and the reliability coefficient are very satisfactory. In 1973 it may be seen that there is still no immediate cause for concern over the test statistics but that, taking the mean and standard deviation into account, it is likely that a number of lower ability candidates are included in the sample. This will, in fact, be seen later to be the case. The percentage of items attempted by 80% of the sample falls to 80·0 in 1973, a fall of 8·8% from the 1968 figure, also indicating the presence of a number of lower ability candidates having problems in coping with the test items.

Table A.2 presents the distribution of the item facilities and item discriminations obtained from the 1 in 20 samples in 1968 and 1973. The item facility is the proportion of the candidates attempting an item who answer it correctly, and the item discrimination is the biserial correlation between the performance of the candidates on an item—considered to be a 'dichotomous' observation of a 'continuous' latent trait—and the performance of the candidates on the test as a whole. (For a discussion of

Table A.2 Distribution of item facilities and item discrimination indices—
1968 and 1973

RANGE	FACILITY		DISCRIMINATION	
	1968	1973	1968	1973
0.00–0.04	–	–	–	–
0.05–0.09	2	2	–	–
0.10–0.14	1	1	–	2
0.15–0.19	–	2	–	–
0.20–0.24	3	4	3	1
0.25–0.29	3	1	1	1
0.30–0.34	4	5	5	2
0.35–0.39	9	10	5	5
0.40–0.44	5	7	12	9
0.45–0.49	6	7	9	5
0.50–0.54	4	5	12	13
0.55–0.59	5	6	23	18
0.60–0.64	5	8	8	14
0.65–0.69	9	7	2	8
0.70–0.74	8	5	–	2
0.75–0.79	5	3	–	–
0.80–0.84	6	4	–	–
0.85–0.89	3	2	–	–
0.90–0.94	2	1	–	–
0.95–1.00	–	–	–	–
TOTAL	80	80	80	80
MEAN	0.55	0.51	0.49	0.52

the relative merits of various item discrimination indices see for example Guilford, 1965.) The figures in Table A.2 reflect the variation in mean score from 1968 to 1973 (cf. Table A.1) and the overall increase in both the reliability coefficient and the standard deviation is reflected by the slightly higher item discrimination indices.

Most of the information concerning the reliability of Test 100 comes from internal consistency estimates relating to various test adminis-trations. In 1968, however, a special exercise was undertaken to study the relationship between Test 100 and its predecessor, CP66. The design of the study was balanced, with 14 schools (837 pupils) taking Test 100 before also taking CP66, and another 14 schools (552 pupils) taking CP 66 before also taking Test 100. The schools were chosen in order that each CSE board was represented in each part of the trial. The correlations between the tests were 0·882 and 0·873 for the two parts of the study (Nuttall, 1971). Remembering that the reliabilities of each test affect the correlation which may be obtained between the two tests, these figures may be considered to be very satisfactory and to be a lower bound estimate of the alternate forms reliability of either test (e.g. Gulliksen, 1950; Guilford, 1965; Lord and Novick, 1968). This fact will be used later when an estimate of the error variance associated with a test score in a regression situation is required.

It is seen, therefore, that Test 100 is a test suited to the population of those pupils in secondary schools taking public examinations in 1968 and 1973; it discriminates between them and is of satisfactory reliability. The question remains, however, as to whether it is measuring anything useful and this aspect of the test is the subject of the following section.

THE CONCURRENT VALIDITY OF TEST 100

To be of any substantial use in studying grades awarded in public examinations, there must be at least some overlap between these grades and the monitoring test used in terms of the trait (or combination of traits) being measured. Table A.3 presents the correlation coefficients between Test 100 scores and the subject grades calculated for each of the CSE and GCE subjects studied in 1968 and 1973. It may be seen that there are a number of quite large values obtained. As the grade scales run contrary to the scale of marks on the test (Grade 1 is the highest achievement whereas a test score of 80 is the highest achievement) all the correlations are negative.

It may be seen from Table A.3 that, in general, the correlations are higher in 1973 than in 1968; this fact is almost certainly due to the wider range of ability of candidates offering themselves for examination in 1973 than was the case in 1968, and is very unlikely to be due to any marked change in the subject content. Not surprisingly, the lowest correlations

Table A.3   Correlations of Test 100 with subject grades for the CSE and GCE sectors—1968 and 1973

SUBJECT	GCE SUBJECTS		CSE SUBJECTS	
	1968	1973	1968	1973
ART	−0.15	−0.24	−0.05	−0.20
BIOLOGY	−0.43	−0.52	−0.44	−0.42
CHEMISTRY	−0.40	−0.52	−0.45	−0.44
DOMESTIC*	−0.28	−	−0.27	−
ENGLISH LANGUAGE	−0.42	−0.47	−0.37	−0.39
FRENCH	−0.32	−0.36	−0.23	−0.26
GENERAL SCIENCE	−0.42	−	−0.51	−
GEOGRAPHY	−0.40	−0.46	−0.42	−0.45
GERMAN	−0.30	−	−0.42	−
HISTORY	−0.29	−0.35	−0.30	−0.36
MATHEMATICS	−0.52	−0.61	−0.61	−0.65
METALWORK	−0.21	−	−0.19	−
NEEDLEWORK	−0.30	−	−0.28	−
PHYSICS	−0.46	−0.56	−0.50	−0.55
R.E.*	−0.22	−	−0.31	−
T.D.*	−0.29	−0.41	−0.40	−0.46
WOODWORK	−0.13	−	−0.27	−
TYPEWRITING	−	−	−0.20	−
ENGLISH LITERATURE	−0.28	−	−	−
P.W.C.*	−0.38	−	−	−
LATIN	−0.22	−	−	−

* DOMESTIC   = Domestic studies
  R.E.   = Religious education
  T.D.   = Technical drawing
  P.W.C.   = Physics with chemistry

are found with the less 'academic' subjects such as art, domestic studies, metalwork, woodwork and typewriting although Latin and religious education also have low entries in Table A.3. The cause of the lack of correlation of Test 100 with Latin grades is probably due to the very restrictive nature of the entry to this subject; this 'selectivity' factor may also be the cause of the rather low value for French in the CSE sector.

It may be argued, however, that many of the values in Table A.3 are surprisingly high. Test 100 was constructed to test verbal and quantitative aptitude and yet this test correlates very reasonably with a number of sets of subject grades. Perhaps this is not over-surprising after all, as 'British psychologists would have little trouble in explaining this phenomenon on the grounds of the all-pervasive general factor of intelligence, contributing in part to the performance in almost any test or examination'—Nuttall (1971); he goes on, 'A further contributing factor is that most examinations require some written work in which verbal skills are assessed to some extent'. Evidence in support of this line of thinking is given by Nuttall, Backhouse and Willmott, (1974), where it is seen that, if the 'common component' of examination grades is correlated with a number of subjects, values of around 0·72 are obtained. This common component (which must include motivation, persistence, general exam-taking ability etc.) also achieves a correlation with Test 100 of about 0·7 (Backhouse, 1973). Given the unlikely event of two completely specific factors causing spurious results, Test 100 is clearly related to a common ability across examinations. Obviously these are persuasive arguments and are ones which are lent support by studies of internal consistency reliability, where a greater degree of homogeneity between marks awarded on questions within a paper (in a given subject) is found than might be expected. A discussion of this point is given in Nuttall and Willmott (1972) and in Willmott and Nuttall (1975). Further, a forthcoming report (Hall, 1975) looks in detail at this very point in an attempt to ascertain more precisely the aspects of human intelligence assessed by Test 100 and by subject grades in public examinations at the age of 16+.

IN CONCLUSION

It has been seen that Test 100 was carefully constructed and attains in practice a satisfactory degree of reliability and discrimination between examination candidates taking CSE and GCE examinations at 16+. The concurrent validity of the test is reasonable, especially for the more 'academic' subjects, and the test fared better in this respect in 1973 than in 1968.

Two important caveats should be entered, however, regarding possible flaws in Test 100. First there appears to be an overall bias in favour of boys as opposed to girls . . . and secondly there is a possible slight verbal bias for girls and a stronger quantitative bias for boys. Both these points are discussed at some length by Nuttall, Backhouse and Willmott (1974) and Hall (1975) and it may be seen in their discussions that these issues are extremely complex. Evidence of bias is also discussed by Forrest (1971) and by Forrest and Smith (1972), also using Test 100. It is not proposed to follow this discussion here but, wherever boys and girls are considered separately, these possible drawbacks in the use of Test 100 will be referred to in more detail.

Appendix B   Technical details of methodology

The method of selecting the sample of pupils for the study has been described in the body of the report. In technical terms the study used a stratified cluster sample of pupils. Each CSE board region constituted a stratum, and thus there were 14 strata; the sampling fraction of first-stage elements (schools) varied from stratum to stratum. Within each stratum, every school (cluster) had the same probability of selection. All children in the school satisfying the criteria laid down in Chapter 1 (those in the correct age group and/or taking at least one GCE or CSE exam) were included in the sample.

This method of sampling has two opposing effects. The effect of stratification is usually to increase the precision of estimates derived from the sample relative to a simple random sample of the same overall size. This effect is most marked when each stratum is relatively homogeneous, but there are noticeable differences in means between strata. This occurs essentially because stratification ensures that every sector of the population is adequately represented. Although this should also be the case with simple random sampling, there is a finite probability that the selected sample will contain, for instance, many members of one sector of the population and few or none from another sector. On the other hand the effect of taking clusters of children, rather than a simple random sample, is usually to decrease the precision of estimates. Again, this effect is greatest when the cluster means are widely spread about the overall mean. This occurs because the scores of a given number of pupils observed within a school (cluster) will not in general be as widely spread as would be the case with a simple random sample of the same number of pupils from the whole population. Cluster sampling will also lead to large standard errors when clusters vary markedly in size. This will usually be the case when considering schools.

Let there be K regions in total, $k = 1, 2, \ldots, K$.
Suppose that there are N_k pupils altogether in region k, and M_k schools in

this region. Suppose further that the sample contains n_k pupils in region k and m_k schools in this region.

The assumption was made that $m_k/M_k = n_k/N_k$ i.e. that the proportion of schools sampled in a region is the same as the proportion of pupils sampled. This is effectively the same as saying that the average size of schools in the sample from region k in terms of the 16+ population is the same as the average for the whole of the region. As was described in Chapter 3, this is not strictly true, as the sample schools tended to be larger than average. However, the assumption is necessary, as the value of N_k was not known. The consequence of the assumption is that the results will tend to overestimate the size of the 16+ age group, and also of sub-groups within the overall group.

Consider one such sub-group, which, following the terminology of Kendall and Stuart (1961), we will call a domain of pupils from each of the K regions, although in special cases (for example, results for a given CSE board) this will not be the case. Suppose we have a particular domain d. Let $N_k^{(d)}$ be the number of pupils in a region falling within domain d, and $n_k^{(d)}$ be the number of pupils in the sample in region k falling in domain d. As all pupils in the 16+ age group within a region have the same chance of being in the sample, it can be shown that $n_k^{(d)}/n_k$ is an unbiased estimate of $N_k^{(d)}/N_k$

i.e.
$$E[n_k^{(d)}/n_k] = N_k^{(d)}/N_k.$$

The Test 100 score ranges from 0 to 80. Let $f_{kp}^{(d)}$ be the number of pupils in the sample falling in region k and domain d and scoring p on the test. Then

$$\sum_{p=0}^{80} f_{kp}^{(d)} = n_k^{(d)}.$$

Also define
$$\sum_{k=1}^{K} N_k = N,$$

$$\sum_{k=1}^{K} N_k^{(d)} = N^{(d)}$$

and
$$\sum_{k=1}^{K} n_k^{(d)} = n^{(d)}$$

If $f_{kp}^{(d)}$ is the observed frequency within a region and domain, we would expect a frequency

$$(N_k^{(d)}/n_k^{(d)})f_{kp}^{(d)} = (N_k/n_k)f_{kp}^{(d)}$$

if we had been able to observe the whole region instead of a sample. This is valid because all schools, and hence all pupils, within a region had the same probability of being included in the sample. Over all regions, we would estimate the frequency of score p as

$$\sum_{k=1}^{K} \frac{N_k}{n_k} f_{kp}^{(d)} \qquad \ldots (1)$$

Summing over all values of p gives an estimate of $N_k^{(d)}$, which we cannot observe directly; this estimated domain size is

$$\sum_{k=1}^{K} \sum_{p=0}^{80} \frac{N_k}{n_k} f_{kp}^{(d)} = \hat{N}^{(d)} \qquad \ldots (2)$$

However, as N_k is not known, we replace N_k/n_k by M_k/m_k, because N_k/n_k is assumed equal to M_k/m_k, and define

$$\hat{\hat{N}}^{(d)} = \sum_{k=1}^{K} \sum_{p=0}^{80} \frac{M_k}{m_k} f_{kp}^{(d)} \qquad \ldots (3)$$

$$\therefore \quad \hat{N}(d) = \sum_{k=1}^{K} \frac{M_k}{m_k} n_k^{(d)}, \text{ since } \sum_{p=0}^{80} f_{kp}^{(d)} = n_k^{(d)}$$

N.B. As $N_k/n_k = N_k^{(d)}/n_k^{(d)}$ in expectation, and using (2)

$$E(\hat{N}^{(d)}) = E\left[\sum_{k=1}^{K} \sum_{p=0}^{80} \frac{N_k}{n_k} f_{kp}^{(d)} \right]$$

$$= E\left[\sum_{k=1}^{K} N_k \frac{n_k^{(d)}}{n_k} \right]$$

$$= \sum_{k=1}^{K} N_k \frac{N_k^{(d)}}{N_k}$$

$$= \sum_{k=1}^{K} N_k^{(d)}$$

$$= N^{(d)} \qquad \text{i.e. the estimator } \hat{N}^{(d)} \text{ is unbiased.}$$

Let μ be the domain mean test score, and suppose we estimate this by

$$\hat{\mu} = \frac{\displaystyle\sum_{k=1}^{K} \sum_{p=0}^{80} \frac{N_k}{n_k} f_{kp}^{(d)} p}{\displaystyle\sum_{k=1}^{K} \sum_{p=0}^{80} \frac{N_k}{n_k} f_{kp}^{(d)}}$$

Kendall and Stuart (1961) show that this is asymptotically an unbiased estimate of μ. A more convenient way of writing $\hat{\mu}$ is

$$\hat{\mu} = \sum_{k=1}^{K} G_k \, \overline{Y}_k^{(d)}$$

where

$$G_k = \frac{\dfrac{N_k}{n_k} n_k^{(d)}}{\displaystyle\sum_{k=1}^{K} \dfrac{N_k}{n_k} n_k^{(d)}}$$

and $\overline{Y}_k^{(d)}$ is the sample estimate of the domain mean within the stratum, i.e.

$$\overline{Y}_k^{(d)} = \frac{\displaystyle\sum_{p=0}^{80} f_{kp}^{(d)} p}{n_k^{(d)}}$$

Again, as the values N_k/n_k are unknown, we replace them with M_k/m_k and let

$$\hat{\mu} = \frac{\displaystyle\sum_{k=1}^{K} \sum_{p=0}^{80} \frac{M_k}{m_k} f_{kp}^{(d)} p}{\displaystyle\sum_{k=1}^{K} \sum_{p=0}^{80} \frac{M_k}{m_k} f_{kp}^{(d)}}$$

$$= \frac{\displaystyle\sum_{k=1}^{K} \frac{M_k}{m_k} n_k^{(d)} \overline{Y}_k^{(d)}}{\displaystyle\sum_{k=1}^{K} \frac{M_k}{m_k} n_k^{(d)}}$$

$$\therefore \quad \hat{\mu} = \sum_{k=1}^{K} W_k \, \overline{Y}_k^{(d)}$$

where

$$W_k = \frac{\dfrac{M_k}{m_k} n_k^{(d)}}{\displaystyle\sum_{k=1}^{K} \dfrac{M_k}{m_k} n_k^{(d)}}$$

$$= \frac{\dfrac{M_k}{m_k} n_k^{(d)}}{\hat{N}^{(d)}} \text{ using (3)}$$

If M_k/m_k is greater (or less) than N_k/m_k by a factor which is the same for all regions, we can write N_k/n_k as $\alpha M_k/m_k$ say. Then W_k has the same form as G_k given earlier, so $\hat{\mu}$ is equivalent to $\hat{\mu}$ and is asymptotically unbiased.

In the case of the whole $16 +$ age group some information is available as to the value of N_k, and so it is possible to investigate the relationship of M_k to N_k. Consider the average school size in one region compared with the average for the schools from that region included in the sample. The ratio of these is then

$$\frac{N_k/M_k}{n_k/m_k} = \frac{N_k}{n_k} \cdot \frac{m_k}{M_k} \qquad \dots (4)$$

which, under the assumption that $N_k/n_k = \alpha M_k/m_k$, becomes $\alpha M_k/m_k \times m_k/M_k = \alpha$. It was found that the ratio (4) varied from 0·86 to 1·08 in this study. This means that the assumption of a constant ratio is not strictly valid. However, the range is not sufficient to indicate that $\hat{\mu}$ is likely to be seriously biased for the purpose of estimation in this study.

Because the method of sampling of schools ensured that schools within each region adequately represented the various schools in that region in terms of type and sex of school, it is unlikely that the situation will be markedly worse for individual subjects.

For many of the domains in which the study was interested, the values of $N_k^{(d)}$, $k = 1, 2, \dots, K$ and $N^{(d)}$ were not available. For instance, the size of the group taking at least one GCE subject would not be available, as the statistics maintained by the GCE boards do not allow calculation of the degree of overlap. However, in certain cases, these values would have been obtainable from sources outside the project. For instance, as noted above, the population sizes for all the $16 +$ age group by region would, in principle, be obtainable from DES statistics. Similarly, total numbers of candidates for a specific CSE subject for one board would be obtainable from the appropriate board. To maintain consistency, however, the multiplier M_k/m_k was used in all cases, even where N_k/n_k would be available. Although this has the possible problem of bias mentioned above, it has the merit of consistency within the study.

The study is concerned explicitly with the range of ability of candidates in particular domains within the $16 +$ age group. For a measure which is normally distributed across the population of interest, the usual measure of range is the variance, or its square root, the standard deviation.

Consider our estimated population for a domain d, which has

$$\hat{N}^{(d)} = \sum_{k=1}^{K} \sum_{p=0}^{80} \frac{M_k}{m_k} f_{kp}^{(d)} \quad \text{members,}$$

$$\sum_{k=1}^{K} \frac{M_k}{m_k} f_{kp}^{(d)}$$

of these having a score of p on Test 100. We have already defined the mean $\hat{\mu}^{(d)}$ of this population, and the natural estimate of the variance is

$$\hat{V} = \left(\sum_{k=1}^{K} \sum_{p=0}^{80} \frac{M_k}{m_k} f_{kp}{}^{(d)} p^2 - \hat{N}^{(d)} (\hat{\mu}^{(d)})^2 \right) \Big/ (\hat{N}^{(d)} - 1)$$

Note that this is an estimate of the population variance, *not* the variance of the estimated mean of the population.

$\hat{V}$ has two main advantages:

  (i) it is comparatively easy to calculate.
  (ii) it gives a value which is obviously related to the estimated distribution of test scores for the relevant domain.

Both $\hat{\mu}$ and $\hat{V}$ are sample estimates of population parameters. As such, each has an associated sampling error attached to it. Suppose we have a simple random sample of size n from a population of size N and from this we estimate a mean $\hat{m}$ and variance $\hat{s}$. Then the variance of $\hat{m}$ is estimated by

$$\frac{\hat{s}}{n} \left(1 - \frac{n}{N} \right) \qquad \qquad \ldots (A)$$

The variance of $\hat{s}$ is estimated by $2\hat{s}^2/(n-1)$, though this is less often of interest.

However, we have a much more complex sampling scheme than simple random sampling and this affects the method of calculating the standard error of $\hat{\mu}$. We cannot use $\hat{V}$ in place of $\hat{s}$ in (A) above for a number of reasons:

  (i) the actual sample size is $n^{(d)}$, not $\hat{N}^{(d)}$ and no account is taken of this.
  (ii) $\hat{V}$ does not take account of the fact that the sample is, in fact, stratified by region; allowing for this should reduce the estimated variance of $\hat{\mu}$.
  (iii) $\hat{V}$ does not take account of the fact that the sample was drawn by randomly sampling unequal sized clusters (i.e. schools) within regions. The effect of this would be to increase the estimated variance of $\hat{\mu}$.

These three effects will be discussed in turn.

(i) Effective sample size
If we ignore the effects due to stratification and clustering, and assume that the sample was drawn with replacement, Kendall and Stuart (1961) show that the estimated variance of $\hat{\mu}^{(d)}$ is given by

$$\hat{V}(\hat{\mu}^{(d)}) = \frac{1}{(N^{(d)})^2 n^{(d)} (n^{(d)} - 1)} \left(\sum_{k=1}^{K} \sum_{p=0}^{80} f_{kp}{}^{(d)} p^2 \cdot \frac{M_k{}^2}{m_k{}^2} - \frac{(N^{(d)})^2}{n^{(d)}} \cdot (\hat{\mu}^{(d)})^2 \right)$$

using M_k/m_k as the probability of inclusion in the sample of a pupil in region k.

The assumption that sampling is with replacement is not strictly valid, but with the fairly low overall sampling fraction, this should not cause great distortion.

Suppose that the sampling fraction is, in fact, the same in all regions. Then $M_k/m_k = \beta$, say, $(k = 1, 2, \ldots, K)$. It follows from this that $N^{(d)}/n^{(d)} = \beta$. The expression above then simplifies to give

$$\hat{V}(\hat{\mu}^{(d)}) = \frac{1}{\beta^2 (n^{(d)})^2 n^{(d)} (n^{(d)} - 1)} \left(\sum_{k=1}^{K} \sum_{p=0}^{80} \beta^2 f_{kp}{}^{(d)} \cdot p^2 - \frac{\beta^2 (n^{(d)})^2}{n^{(d)}} \cdot (\hat{\mu}^{(d)})^2 \right)$$

$$= \frac{1}{(n^{(d)})^3 (n^{(d)} - 1)} \left(\sum_{k=1}^{K} \sum_{p=0}^{80} f_{kp}{}^{(d)} p^2 - n^{(d)} (\hat{\mu}^{(d)})^2 \right)$$

which is independent of the sampling fraction.

Under the same assumption of equal sampling fractions, the estimated variance of the population derived earlier reduces to

$$\hat{V} = \frac{1}{\beta n^{(d)} - 1} \left(\sum_{k=1}^{K} \sum_{p=0}^{80} \beta f_{kp} p^2 - \beta n^{(d)} (\hat{\mu}^{(d)})^2 \right)$$

$$= \frac{\beta}{(\beta n^{(d)} - 1)} \left(\sum_{k=1}^{K} \sum_{p=0}^{80} f_{kp}{}^{(d)} p^2 - n^{(d)} (\hat{\mu}^{(d)})^2 \right) \bigg/ (\beta n^{(d)} - 1)$$

Therefore
$$\hat{V}(\hat{\mu}^{(d)}) / \hat{V} = (\beta n^{(d)} - 1) / (n^{(d)})^3 (n^{(d)} - 1) \beta$$
$$\approx \beta n^{(d)} / (n^{(d)})^3 n^{(d)} \beta$$
$$\approx 1 / (n^{(d)})^3$$

Then
$$\hat{V}(\hat{\mu}^{(d)}) \approx 1 / (n^{(d)})^3 \hat{V}$$

This gives an *approximate* relationship between the variance calculated from the predicted distribution, $\hat{V}$, and the variance of the mean. Values of the variance calculated by this method should be treated only as guides to the true value.

The average sampling fraction is 1 in 20, i.e. $\beta \approx 20$, but there are wide variations about this value.

(ii) Effect of stratification by region
As mentioned earlier, stratification usually leads to a decrease in the standard errors of estimates. In this study, each stratum is one CSE region, an area defined on a geographical basis. The gain in precision using geographical stratification is not usually very large; see, for instance, Cochran (1963).

For some of the domains of interest in this study, it is possible to obtain a crude estimate of the effect of stratification. Such domains are the results for the whole CSE sector, where, as noted in Chapter 2, the sector result is obtained by combining results for each board.

In particular, consider results for the whole 16+ age range. In this case, the standard error of the mean is reduced from about 0·1 points of Test 100 scores, ignoring the effect of stratification, to about 0·01 points of score, when stratification is allowed for—a factor of about 10. As will be seen later, although large, this effect is likely to be nullified by the counteracting increase in variance due to cluster sampling.

From the results obtained for this study it is not possible to see how general a reduction of 90% in the standard errors due to stratification might be. However, when looking at specific subjects, the differences between regions is likely to be less than for the whole age group. This is the case because entering for a specific subject is usually dependent on ability, for example, high ability pupils are more likely to attempt German, and less academically inclined pupils to attempt art. This may well mean that a reduction to a tenth of the value of standard errors obtained, ignoring stratifications, is the maximum that would have been gained had stratification been allowed for in the calculations.

(iii)   Effect of clustering by school

It was indicated earlier that the effect of using a cluster sample is usually to increase the variance of sample estimates. The calculation of the variance of the mean for a cluster sample involves finding the mean and variance separately for each school for each table. Such calculations, in general, were beyond the resources of the project. However, it was possible to consider one simple case to try to estimate the magnitude of the effect. All pupils in one CSE region who took Test 100 were included. In this case, ignoring the effect of clustering leads to a standard error approximately 15 times too small.

That is, the effect is of broadly the same magnitude, but in the opposite direction to, that due to stratification. There is no reason to believe that the region used for this example is likely to produce results markedly different from those for any other region. As with stratification, the selection effect applying to a given subject may mean that the ratio of 15 is an overestimate of what would be obtained: clusters of pupils taking the same subject are likely to be closer in mean score than pupils in general. Also, because schools will usually enter either no pupils or a reasonable number of pupils for a given subject such clusters will tend to be closer in size than for pupils in general.

As a very crude approximation, it seems that the effects of stratification and clustering counteract each other and can be ignored.

THE AGE EFFECT IN TEST 100

For computational convenience, results were first obtained within each CSE region. For all candidates in the sample entered for at least one GCE examination who were younger than the 16+ age group, the mean and standard deviation of the Test 100 scores were calculated as was the mean age. (No weighting was necessary because this was carried out within a CSE region.) Similar calculations were carried out for all 16+ students who had previously entered at least one GCE. Comparison of the two groups showed that, as expected, the mean ages differed by approximately 12 months.

For the whole of the 16+ age group, the gradient obtained by regressing the Test 100 score on age in months was calculated. Using the whole group enables a better estimate to be obtained, as the sample size is much larger, and it was not expected that there would be differences in gradient (though, of course, differences in mean score would be expected) between 16+ pupils who had and had not attempted GCE early.

These gradients were then weighted and pooled across all CSE regions to give an estimate of the population gradient; this was calculated to be about 0·278 points of score for each month of age or approximately 3·3 points of score for each year of age.

The assumption of a linear relationship between test score and age is unlikely to be valid for a large age range, but is a reasonable approximation for a one-year band, such as considered here. However, the actual correlation of test score with age was, in general, very small—in most regions being less than 0·1.

Because the age correction would be small and with a comparatively high standard error, and also because comparatively few pupils would be affected, it was decided that the extra complexity which would be introduced by age-correcting Test 100 scores was not justified.

Appendix C   Syllabus titles and subject reference codes

The following abbreviations are used to designate examining boards in Appendix C

NAME OF GCE BOARD

Associated Examining Board	**A**
University of Cambridge Local Examinations Syndicate	**C**
Joint Matriculation Board	**J**
Oxford Delegacy of Local Examinations	**O**
Oxford and Cambridge Schools Examination Board	**OC**
Southern Universities Joint Board	**SU**
University of London Schools Examinations Department	**L**
Northern Ireland Schools Examinations Council	**IG**
Welsh Joint Education Committee	**WG**

NAME OF CSE BOARD

Associated Lancashire Schools Examining Board	**AL**
East Anglian Examinations Board	**E**
East Midland Regional Examinations Board	**EM**
Metropolitan Regional Examinations Board	**ME**
Middlesex Regional Examining Board	**MI**
North Regional Examinations Board	**N**
North Western Secondary School Examinations Board	**NW**
South East Regional Examinations Board	**SE**
Southern Regional Examinations Board	**S**
South Western Examinations Board	**SW**
West Yorkshire and Lindsey Regional Examining Board	**WY**
Yorkshire Regional Examinations Board	**Y**
West Midlands Examinations Board	**WM**
Northern Ireland Schools Examinations Council	**IC**
Welsh Joint Education Committee	**WC**

Subject code Ref. No. Name	Title of syllabus	Used in board GCE	CSE
1　**Arts and crafts**	Art	**L J O C WG OC A**	**N SW AL MI**
	Art I and II (painting)	**SU**	
	Art I and III (crafts)	**SU**	
	Art and associated crafts		**MI**
	Art and craft		**S E WM EM**
	Art and crafts	**A**	**SE WY**
	Art, craft and design		**EM**
	Art and design		**WC Y ME NW E WY**
	Craft (design and practice)	**J**	
	Crafts	**WG A**	
	Handicraft (creative embroidery)	**L**	
	History of art	**A**	
	Pottery	**O**	
	Art 16+	**J**	**AL**
	Art and design 16+		**NW**
	Printing and bookbinding		**SE**
2　**British constitution**	British constitution	**L O WG A**	**SW**

Subject code Ref. No. Name	Title of syllabus	Used in board GCE	CSE
3 **Civics**	Civics		**SE S Y**
	Citizenship		**SW**
	Government and citizenship		**NW**
	Government and public affairs		**E**
	Business and public affairs		**E**
4 **Classical studies**	Classical studies	**J**	**E EM WM WY SW**
	Classical studies B		**WC**
	Classics in translation	**C**	
	Greek lit. in translation	**L O**	
	Greek and Roman lit. in translation	**WG**	
	Classical Greek/ Roman civilization	**SU C L OC**	
	Classical studies (JAVT)	**OC**	
	Classical studies 16+	**J**	
5 **Classics with or without Latin**	Classical studies		**ME MI NW WC**
6 **Greek**	Greek	**L J O C WG OC SU**	

Subject code Ref. No. Name	Title of syllabus	Used in board GCE	CSE
7 Latin	Latin	**L J O C WG OC A SU**	
	Latin (SCP)	**L O A**	
	Latin 16+	**J**	**Y AL WY**
8 Latin or Greek with classical studies	General classics	**OC**	
	Greek with classical studies	**J**	
	Latin with classical studies	**J**	**E**
	Latin		**SW EM WY**
	Classical studies with Latin		**WM**
	Classical studies A		**WC**
	Greek		**WY**
	Latin, Roman life and lit.		**AL**
9 Accounts	Accounts		**EM WM Y AL WY SW**
	Book-keeping and accounting	**J**	
	Elements of accounts		**N**
	Principles of accounts	**L O C WG A SU**	**S E WC ME MI NW**
	Book-keeping		**WY**

Subject code Ref. No. Name	Title of syllabus	Used in board GCE	CSE
10 Commerce	Commerce	**L O C WG A SU**	**SE N S E WC EM WM SW Y AL ME MI NW WY**
	Social economics		**E**
11 Office practice	Office practice		**S E WC EM SW Y ME WY**
	Business studies		**SE**
	Clerical duties		**WY**
	Office studies		**WY**
12 Shorthand	Shorthand		**N S EM AL★ NW★ WY E★ WC★ Y★ MI★**
	Elements of shorthand		**EM**
	Shorthand speed		**EM★**
	Shorthand and allied systems		**WM**
	Theory of shorthand		**E**
13 Typewriting	Typewriting		**N S E WC★ EM WM SW Y AL MI NW WY**
	Typewriting with office practice		**ME**

★Only speeds given, not included in analysis

Subject code Ref. No. Name	Title of syllabus	Used in board GCE	CSE
	Audio-display typewriting		**E**
	Audio-typing		**EM**
14 Cookery	Cookery	**C WG SU**	**Y**
	Domestic science (food)	**J**	
	Domestic science/ cookery	**O**	
	Food and nutrition	**L**	
	Nutrition and cookery	**A**	
15 Home economics	Home economics		**N S WC WM SW Y AL MI WY**
	Homecraft		**EM AL NW WY**
	Homemaking		**SE NW**
	Housecraft		**ME WY**
	Domestic science		**E NW Y WY**
	Cook and hostess		**SE**
	Housecraft 16+		**WY**
16 Housecraft	Housecraft	**WG**	
	Domestic science/ housecraft	**O**	
	Domestic science	**OC**	
	General housecraft	**C**	

Subject code Ref. No. Name	Title of syllabus	Used in board GCE	CSE
17 Needlework	Domestic science (clothing)	**J**	
	Domestic science/ needlework	**O**	
	Dress	**A**	**E EM**
	Dress and needlecraft		**Y**
	Dressmaking	**WG**	
	Embroidery	**A**	**SE E EM NW**
	Embroidery and design		**ME**
	Fashion		**SE**
	Fashion and clothing		**AL**
	Needlecraft	**SU**	**E WM SW ME NW WY**
	Needlecraft (dress)		**MI**
	Needlecraft and dress	**L**	
	Needlework		**N S WC MI WY**
	Needlework (dress)		**S**
	Needlework and dressmaking	**C**	
	Needlework and dressmaking 16+	**C**	

| Subject code | | Title of syllabus | Used in board | |
| Ref. | | | GCE | CSE |
No.	Name			
17	**Needlework (Cont.)**	Needlework 16+		**E**
		Needlecraft and design		**Y**
18	**Economics**	Economics	**L O WG**	**EM SW Y AL NW**
		Economic principles	**A**	
		Social economics	**A**	**WY**
		Elements of economics		**MI**
19	**Economics and government**	Economics and public affairs	**C SU**	**NW**
		Government economics and commerce	**J**	
		Institutional studies	**O**	
20	**English**	English	**A**	**SE S E WC EM WM Y AL ME MI NW WY**
		English A		**SW**
		English B		**SW**
		English language and lit.		**N MI WY**
		English 16+		**AL WY**

| Subject code | | Title of syllabus | Used in board | |
| Ref. | | | GCE | CSE |
No.	Name			
21	**English language**	English language	**L J O WG OC A SU**	**WM**
		English language— written		**N**
		English language—oral		**N**
		English language 16+	**J**	**WM**
		English studies— language		**WM**
22	**English literature**	English literature	**L J O C WG OC A SU**	**N WC WM SW NW AL WY**
		English literature		**WM**
		English lit. 16+	**J**	**WM**
		English lit. (general)	**O**	
		English lit. (selected)	**O**	
23	**Geography**	Geography	**L J O C WG OC A SU**	**SE N S E WC EM WM Y AL ME MI NW WY SW**
		Geography 16+	**L J C WG**	**E WC Y AL NW**
		Geography schools project	**A**	

Subject code Ref. No. Name	Title of syllabus	Used in board GCE	CSE
24 Geology	Geology	**L J O WG A SU**	**WC EM WM SW N MI WY**
25 History	History	**L J C WG OC A SU**	**S E N S E WC EM WM SW AL ME NW WY MI**
	History (social and economic)		**Y**
	History (British)	**O**	
	History—British soc. and economic	**O**	
	History—British economic	**L**	
	History— economic	**A**	
	History—Brit. Emp. Commonwealth	**O**	
	History—British and foreign	**O**	
	History—foreign	**O**	
	History— American	**O**	
	History—world (in 20th century)	**O A**	
	History—modern world		**Y**
	History 16+	**J O**	**S WM**
	World history		**S**

| Subject code | | Title of syllabus | Used in board | |
Ref. No.	Name		GCE	CSE
25	**History (cont.)**	World affairs since 1919		**ME**
26	**History— Ancient**	Ancient history	**OC L**	
		Greek and Roman history	**WG**	
27	**Mathematics**	Maths	**L J O C WG OC A SU**	**SE N S E WC EM WM SW Y AL ME MI NW WY**
		Alternative maths		**N**
		Maths A (alternative)		**SW**
		Modern maths		**AL**
		Maths 16+	**WG A**	**WC MI**
		Maths MME	**A**	
		SMP maths		**MI**
28	**Maths additional**	Additional maths	**L O C WG OC A**	**Y**
		Further maths		**MI**
		Applied maths		**MI**
		Additional statistics	**A**	
		Statistics	**WG A**	**MI**
		Additional maths MEi	**L**	
		Additional maths SMP	**L O**	

| Subject code | | Title of syllabus | Used in board | |
| Ref. | | | GCE | CSE |
No.	Name			
29	**Maths, commercial/ arithmetic**	Arithmetic		**SE MI WC S Y AL WY**
		Certificate in arithmetic	**C A SU**	
		Commercial maths	**J**	**WY**
		Commercial arith. and stats.		**NW**
		Commercial arithmetic		**EM**
		Commercial calculation		**S**
		Maths and stats. for commerce	**SU**	
		Calculations		**E**
		Commercial maths with stats.		**AL**
		Social arithmetic		**NW**
30	**Maths SMP**	Maths SMP	**L J O C OC A**	
31	**French**	French	**L J O C WG OC A SU**	**SE N S E WC EM WM SW Y AL ME MI MW WY**
		French 16+	**J O**	**S AL**
		French Nuffield	**O**	

| Subject code | | Title of syllabus | Used in board | |
Ref. No.	Name		GCE	CSE
32	**German**	German	L J O C WG OC A SH	SE N S E WC EM WM SW Y AL ME MI NW WY
33	**Italian**	Italian	L J O C WG OC A SU	SW Y WC
34	**Russian**	Russian	L J O C WG OC A SU	E SW Y WY EM S
35	**Spanish**	Spanish	L J O C WG OC A SU	N S E WC EM WM AL ME MI NW SW
36	**Welsh**	Welsh	O OC	
		Welsh 03	WG	WC
37	**Welsh lang. literature**	Welsh language	WG	
		Welsh lit. 01	WG	WC
		Welsh 02	WG	WC
		Welsh literature		WC
		Welsh	J	
38	**Irish**	Irish	A	
39	**Music**	Music	L J O C WG OC A SU	SE N S E WC EM WM SW Y AL ME MI NW WY
		History and appreciation of music	J	

Subject code Ref. No. Name	Title of syllabus	Used in board GCE	CSE
40 Religious studies	Religious and moral studies		**Y**
	Religious education		**AL E WM SW Y NW**
	Moral education		**AL**
	Religious studies	**L J O C A**	**SE S ME**
	Religious knowledge	**OC SU**	**N EM AL MI WY**
	Scripture	**WG**	
	Scripture knowledge		**WC**
41 Rural studies	Rural studies		**SE N S E EM SW Y AL NW WY**
	Rural science		**WC WM**
	Agricultural and horticultural studies		**E**
	Agricultural studies		**Y WY**
	Agriculture		**WY**
42 Agricultural science	Agricultural science	**O C WG**	
	Horticultural science	**WG**	
	Rural biology (agri.)	**J**	

Subject code Ref. No. Name	Title of syllabus	Used in board GCE	CSE
42 Agricultural science (cont.)	Rural biology (hort.)	J	
43 Biology	Biology	L J O C WG OC A SU	SE N S E WC EM WM SW Y AL ME MI NW WY
	Biology 16+	C A	E ME WY
	Science (biology)		EM
44 Biology human	Human biology	L O WG A SU	N S E WC WM SW Y ME MI NW
	Human and social biology		AL
	Science of living		SE
	Health education		NW
	Human biology and health education		AL
	Health		AL
	Human biology and public health		WY
	Nursing studies		WY
	Nursing		WY
45 Biology, Nuffield	Biology, Nuffield	J O OC A	
46 Botany	Botany	L O WG OC	

Subject code Ref. No. Name	Title of syllabus	Used in board GCE	CSE
47 **Chemistry**	Chemistry	**L J O C** **WG OC A** **SU**	**SE N S E** **WC EM WM** **SW Y AL** **ME MI NW** **WY**
	Chemistry 16+	**L J**	**WM Y**
	Environmental chemistry		**WY**
48 **Chemistry, Nuffield**	Nuffield chemistry	**L J O C A**	
49 **Engineering science**	Engineering science	**L C WG**	**SE MI NW** **AL WY**
	Science, building and engineering	**A**	
	Technical science	**J**	
	Engineering	**MI**	
50 **General science**	General science	**L J O WG** **A SU OC**	**N S E WC** **EM WM SW** **Y AL MI WY**
	Science		**NW Y**
	Integrated science	**L A**	**SE Y MI WY**
	Science (combined science)		**EM**
	Integrated studies science		**SW**

Subject code Ref. No. Name	Title of syllabus	Used in board GCE	CSE
51 **Physics**	Physics	**L J O C WG OC A SU**	**SE N S E WC EM WM SW Y AL ME MI NW WY**
	Physics 16+	**O**	**S NW**
	Practical physics		**NW**
	Technical physics		**WY**
52 **Physics, Nuffield**	Physics, Nuffield	**L J O C A**	
53 **Physics with chemistry**	Physics with chemistry	**L J O OC A SU**	**N E EM Y WY**
	Physical science	**J C WG**	
	Physics, Nuffield with London chemistry	**L**	
	Physics with chemistry, all Nuffield	**L O**	
54 **Social studies**	Social studies		**SE E EM ME MI N S Y AL NW WY**
	Sociology	**A O**	**SE S Y WY**
	The living community		**S**
	Social and environmental studies		**E**

Subject code Ref. No. Name	Title of syllabus	Used in board	
		GCE	CSE
	Community studies		**EM AL**
	Urban studies		**Y**
	Child dev. and the family		**ME**
	Social education		**ME**
	Community living		**ME**
55 Craftwork	Craftwork		**AL**
	Craftwork and design	**A**	
	Craft technology		**S**
	Design and technology	**L**	
56 Engineering workshop theory and practice	Eng. wkshp. theory and practice	**J O WG A**	**E NW MI WY**
	Engineering studies		**ME E EM**
	Engineering metalwork		**WY**
	Metalwork (eng.)	**C**	
	Technical studies— engineering		**N**
	Engineering		**AL**
	Engineering workshop		**NW**

Subject code Ref. No. Name	Title of syllabus	Used in board GCE	CSE
57 Metalwork	Metalwork	**J O C WG OC SU**	**SE N S E WC EM WM SW Y AL ME MI NW WY**
	Craftwork—metal	**A**	
	Metalcraft		**WY**
	Metalwork (art)		**MI**
58 Technical drawing	Geometry and building drawing	**C WG**	**N E NW**
	Geom. and eng. drawing	**J WG OC**	**E NW WY**
	Geom. and machine drawing	**SU**	
	Geom. and mechanical drawing	**C**	
	Geom. and technical drawing		**WY**
	Geom. and woodwork drawing		**NW**
	Geom. drawing (build.)	**A**	
	Geom. drawing (eng.)	**A**	**WM**
	Engineering drawing	**O**	**N WM**

Subject code Ref. No. Name	Title of syllabus	Used in board GCE	CSE
58 **Technical drawing (cont.)**	Technical drawing		**SE N S E WC EM WM SW Y AL ME MI NW WY**
	Technical drawing (cons.)	**O**	
	Technical drawing (eng.)	**L**	
	Building construction and geom. drawing		**AL**
	Technical drawing 16+	**C**	**WY**
	Graphical communication 16+	**L**	**ME**
59 **Woodwork**	Woodwork	**J O C WG OC SU**	**SE N S E WC EM WM SW Y AL ME MI NW WY**
	Craftwork—wood	**A**	
60 **Arts (humanities etc.)**	Law	**O**	
	Law and constitution	**A**	
	European studies		**SE EM**
	Drama		**N WC WM SW Y AL MI NW WY**

Subject board Ref. No. Name	Title of syllabus	Used in board GCE	CSE
60 **Arts** **(humanities** **etc.) (cont.)**	Related studies— history and geography		**N**
	Humanities		**S E SW Y** **AL NW WY**
	British political history		**S**
	Welsh studies		**WC**
	Geography with commerce		**WM**
	History with geography		**WM**
	Social economics		**WM**
	Social education		**WM**
	Social studies		**WM**
	English		**WM**
	Film studies		**SW**
	Use of English	**C**	**Y**
	Creative drama and stage technique		**AL**
	Latin		**AL**
	History of British drama and stagecraft		**AL**
	General principles of English law	**A**	
	Spoken English	**L**	

Subject code Ref. No. Name	Title of syllabus	Used in board GCE	CSE
61 Arts and crafts/ music	Photography		**N SW MI**
	Art, photography		**WM**
	Art and craft		**WM**
	Creative arts		**WM**
	Art and design		**WM**
	Craft and creative use of materials		**AL**
	Craft		**NW**
	Design for living		**WY**
62 Commercial subjects	Commercial studies		**WC WY**
	Shorthand/typing		**MI**
	Commercial arith. and accounts	**O**	
	Commercial practice and office organization		**N**
	Office studies		**E**
	Business studies— office practice with audio- typing		**AL**
	Business studies— office practice with typing		**AL**
	Commerce for the consumer		**ME**

Subject code Ref. No. Name	Title of syllabus	Used in board GCE	CSE
62 Commercial subjects (cont.)	Office practice		**MI**
	Commerce and typewriting		**NW**
	Business studies		**WY**
	Commercial services		**WY**
	Typing and office practice		**WY**
63 Domestic subjects	Child care		**SE WY**
	Home maintenance		**S**
	Home and child welfare		**E**
	Household design and furnishing		**E**
	Nutrition		**WC**
	Catering		**EM**
	Needlework with art and craft		**WM**
	Home econ. home and the community		**WM**
	Home economics with needlework		**WM**
	Science: catering		**AL**
	Basic catering		**ME**
	Catering practice and organization		**ME**
	Cookery and entertaining		**MI**

Subject code Ref. No. Name	Title of syllabus	Used in board GCE	CSE
64 **Maths**	Computer studies	**A**	**N WM E SW Y AL ME**
	Logic	**L**	
	Navigation	**L A J O**	
	Navigation and astronomy	**C**	
	Astronomy	**L**	
	Maths for biology	**J**	
	Computer science	**J WG**	**SE**
	Mathematics		**WM**
	Elementary mathematics		**WM**
	Statistics		**ME**
	Practical drawing and arithmetic		**NW**
65 **Modern languages**	Use of English for immigrants		**WM**
	Polish	**L J C**	
	Swedish	**L O**	
	Gujerati	**L**	
	Urdu	**L**	
	Persian	**L O**	
	Hindu	**L**	
	Greek (modern)	**L OC**	
	Portuguese	**L**	

Subject code Ref. No. Name	Title of syllabus	Used in board GCE	CSE
65 Modern languages (cont.)	Malay	**L**	
	Norwegian	**L**	
	Turkish	**L**	
	Swahili	**L O**	
	Arabic	**L**	
	Serbo-Croat	**J O**	
	Ukranian	**J**	
	Chinese	**J O**	
	Dutch	**C OC A**	
	Modern Hebrew	**OC**	
	Afrikaans	**A**	
	French studies		**Y AL WY**
66 Science subjects	Biology with physics	**O**	
	Biological science		**S WY**
	Chemistry with biology	**O**	
	Combined science		**S**
	Environmental science	**C**	**ME NW**
	Environmental studies	**L O**	**E SE N S EM Y AL NW WY**
	General science additional	**L**	
	Horticulture		**WC**
	Natural science		**ME**

Subject code Ref. No. Name	Title of syllabus	Used in board GCE	CSE
66 Science subjects (cont.)	Physical science	**A**	**S SW MI WY**
	Zoology	**L**	
	Science (double subject)	**J**	
	Building services engineering		**EM**
	Human biology with chemistry		**WM**
	Human biology with rural science		**WM**
	Materials science		**WM**
	Physics with rural science		**WM**
	Chemistry		**WM**
	Earth sciences		**WM**
	Integrated biology		**ME**
	Modern science		**ME**
	Scientific studies		**NW**
	Science		**WY**
67 Technical subjects	Building construction	**A**	
	Building crafts	**A**	
	Building practice	**A**	**WY**
	Building studies		**ME SE N E**
	Motor engineering		**ME E SW WY**

Subject code Ref. No. Name	Title of syllabus	Used in board GCE	CSE
67 **Technical subjects (cont.)**	Surveying	**L J C A**	**SE AL**
	Elements of engineering design	**C**	
	Textiles	**J**	**AL**
	Principles of building construction and design	**J**	
	Applied science-technology	**O**	
	Automobile eng.		**SE E WM**
	Applied 3-dimen. design		**SE**
	Electronic eng. and communication		**SE**
	Building craft practice		**SE**
	Electrical engineering		**SE AL WY**
	Mechanical and electrical eng. craft practice		**SE**
	Electrical technology		**SE**
	Mech. eng.		**SE**
	Construction practice		**SE**
	Related studies, craft		**N**

Subject code Ref. No. Name	Title of syllabus	Used in board GCE	CSE
67 Technical subjects (cont.)	Motor vehicle maintenance		**S**
	Electronics		**E WM SW**
	Building crafts		**E**
	Technical studies		**SW Y WY**
	Vehicle body repair work		**E**
	Welding		**E**
	Motor mechanics		**E**
	Brickwork		**WC EM**
	Carpentry, joinery and machine woodworking		**WC**
	Automobile mechanics		**WC**
	Carpentry and joinery		**EM**
	Electrical installation		**EM**
	Motor vehicle technology		**EM**
	Woodwork with TD		**WM**
	Technology		**SW NW WY**
	Integrated practical studies		**Y**
	Basic technology		**AL**
	Building		**AL**

Subject code Ref. No. Name	Title of syllabus	Used in board GCE	CSE
67 Technical subjects (cont.)	Building (professional)		**AL**
	Building (craft)		**AL**
	Technical studies electronics		**AL**
	Technical studies building materials		**Al**
	Building painting and decorating		**AL**
	Technical studies eng. materials		**AL**
	Control technology		**AL WY**
	Motor vehicle studies		**MI**
	Integrated crafts		**NW**
	Handicraft		**WY**
	General technical studies		**WY**
	Motor technology		**WY**
	Motor vehicle craft		**WY**
	Eng. technology		**WY**
	Craft studies		**WY**
68 Others	Seamanship	**C**	
	Nautical studies		**E**
	Hebrew (classical)	**L**	

Subject code Ref. No. Name	Title of syllabus	Used in board GCE	CSE
68 Others (cont.)	Design	**O**	
	3D studies craft design	**WG**	
	Technical service	**A**	
	History of English agriculture		**SE**
	Dinghy sailing and seamanship		**SE**
	Community service		**SE**
	Related studies— motor vehicle science		**N**
	Related studies— design		**N**
	Technical studies—applied science		**N**
	Art of movement		**E**
	Combined crafts		**WC**
	Local studies		**EM**
	Metals and modern materials		**EM**
	Contemporary studies		**EM**
	Education for living		**WM**

Subject code Ref. No. Name	Title of syllabus	Used in board	
		GCE	CSE
	Environmental studies		**WM**
	Textile craft		**WM**
	Rural technology		**WM**
	Commerce with accounts		**WM**
	Modern studies		**Y AL MI**
	General studies		**Y WY**
	Library studies		**AL**
	Business studies— library		**AL**
	Local studies		**AL**
	Kent studies		**ME**
	Dance		**ME**
	Community education		**MI**
	Embroidery and design		**MI**
	Practical housecraft		**WY**
	Materials		**WY**
	Community studies		**WY**

Appendix D   Tables of estimates of 16+ age group population

Table D.1   The actual sample of pupils with Test 100 scores by year group

CSE BOARD	16+ Age Group				Young Candidates			
	School Year Group							
	4th	5th	6th	Total	4th	5th	6th	Total
11	3	1819	83	1905	248	84	–	332
12	6	2136	13	2155	7	28	–	35
13	11	2128	92	2231	326	76	1	403
14	4	2421	52	2477	46	40	1	87
15	1	2220	15	2236	77	13	–	90
16	9	2215	29	2253	85	18	–	103
17	–	2184	15	2199	80	20	–	100
18	–	2208	52	2260	36	68	1	105
19	4	2485	61	2550	88	43	1	132
20	9	1978	163	2150	233	26	–	259
21	4	2071	43	2118	197	34	–	231
22	33	1749	56	1838	112	54	–	166
23	–	1877	65	1942	53	30	2	85
24	7	2403	14	2424	185	38	–	223
TOTAL	91	29894	753	30738	1773	572	6	2351

Table D.2 Absentees and remedial pupils in the sample schools by year group

CSE BOARD	ABSENTEES				REMEDIALS
	4th	5th	6th	Total	5th Only
11	5	128	11	144	9
12	1	127	-	128	-
13	15	124	-	139	28
14	-	300	1	301	8
15	1	479	-	480	9
16	-	166	2	168	6
17	2	221	-	223	27
18	-	223	1	224	11
19	3	279	1	283	14
20	6	339	2	347	40
21	5	562	3	570	119
22	-	273	1	274	18
23	-	161	2	163	15
24	6	219	1	226	7
TOTAL	44	3601	25	3670	311

Table D.3 Estimates of the 16 + age group population by year group

CSE BOARD	No. of Pupils with Test Score			No. of Recorded Absentee and Remedial			Discrepancy	Total
	School Year Group							
	4th	5th	6th	4th	5th	6th		
11	81	49113	2241	2	3535	297	−759	56028
12	126	44856	273	10	2635	−	−186	48084
13	286	55328	2392	13	3816	−	−903	62738
14	132	79893	1716	−	9999	32	−1021	92793
15	16	35520	240	−	7762	−	−123	43661
16	216	53160	696	−	4095	48	−367	58582
17	−	72072	495	−	8110	−	+63	80614
18	−	46368	1092	−	4767	21	−642	52890
19	44	27335	671	1	3168	11	−241	31471
20	72	15824	1304	2	2993	16	−57	20268
21	56	28994	602	1	9380	42	−366	39441
22	297	15741	504	−	2540	9	−124	19215
23	−	65695	2275	−	6063	68	−34	74135
24	105	36045	210	3	3337	15	−192	39907
TOTAL	1431	625944	14711	32	72198	559	4952	719827

Appendix E   Estimated numbers (and proportions) of pupils in the 16+ age group who enter particular subjects in the CSE or the GCE sector before the end of the school year in which they have their sixteenth birthday—for total sample (1974)

The following is the order in which the subjects appear:

Art
Biology
Chemistry
Classical studies
Commerce
English language
English literature
English
French
German
Geography
History
Housecraft
Mathematics
Music
Physics
Religions studies
Social studies
Technical drawing
Woodwork

SUBJECT: ART

	Not entered CSE in the subject	Entered for CSE in the subject	
Not entered for GCE in the subject	463021 71.5%	107852 16.7%	570873 88.1%
Entered for GCE in the subject	62043 9.6%	14641 2.2%	76684 11.8%
	525064 81.1%	122493 18.9%	647557 100%

SUBJECT: BIOLOGY

	Not entered CSE in the subject	Entered for CSE in the subject	
Not entered for GCE in the subject	399158 61.6%	105900 16.4%	505058 78.0%
Entered for GCE in the subject	127798 19.7%	14701 2.3%	142499 22.0%
	526956 81.3%	120601 18.7%	647557 100%

SUBJECT: CHEMISTRY

	Not entered CSE in the subject	Entered for CSE in the subject	
Not entered for GCE in the subject	505240 78.0%	51114 7.9%	556354 85.9%
Entered for GCE in the subject	82980 12.8%	8223 1.3%	91203 14.1%
	588220 90.8%	59337 9.2%	647557 100%

SUBJECT: CLASSICAL STUDIES

	Not entered CSE in the subject	Entered for CSE in the subject	
Not entered for GCE in the subject	600106 92.7%	3256 0.5%	603362 93.2%
Entered for GCE in the subject	44069 6.8%	126 0.0%	44195 6.8%
	644175 99.5%	3382 0.5%	647557 100%

SUBJECT: COMMERCE

	Not entered CSE in the subject	Entered for CSE in the subject	
Not entered for GCE in the subject	613218 94.7%	28495 4.4%	641713 99.1%
Entered for GCE in the subject	4236 0.7%	1608 0.2%	5844 0.9%
	617454 95.4%	30103 4.6%	647557 100%

SUBJECT: ENGLISH LANGUAGE ‡

	Not entered CSE in the subject	Entered for CSE in the subject	
Not entered for GCE in the subject	330935 51.1%	31699 4.9%	362634 56.0%
Entered for GCE in the subject	281105 43.4%	3818 0.6%	284923 44.0%
	612040 94.5%	35517 5.5%	647557 100%

‡   this specifically excludes CSE English involving a component of Literature.

SUBJECT: ENGLISH LITERATURE

	Not entered CSE in the subject	Entered for CSE in the subject	
Not entered for GCE in the subject	378635 58.5%	64181 9.9%	442816 68.4%
Entered for GCE in the subject	201724 31.1%	3017 0.5%	204741 31.6%
	580359 89.6%	67198 10.4%	647557 100%

SUBJECT: ENGLISH

	Not entered CSE in the subject	Entered for CSE in the subject	
Not entered for GCE in the subject	116696 18.0%	239696 37.0%	356392 55.0%
Entered for GCE in the subject	234217 36.2%	56948 8.8%	291165 45.0%
	350913 54.2%	296644 45.8%	647557 100%

SUBJECT: FRENCH

	Not entered CSE in the subject	Entered for CSE in the subject	
Not entered for GCE in the subject	417224 64.4%	84682 13.1%	501906 77.5%
Entered for GCE in the subject	136616 21.1%	9035 1.4%	145651 22.5%
	553840 85.5%	93717 14.5%	647557 100%

SUBJECT: GERMAN

	Not entered CSE in the subject	Entered for CSE in the subject	
Not entered for GCE in the subject	592808 91.6%	15844 2.4%	576964 94.0%
Entered for GCE in the subject	36342 5.6%	2563 0.4%	38905 6.0%
	629150 97.2%	18407 2.8%	647557 100%

SUBJECT: GEOGRAPHY

	Not entered CSE in the subject	Entered for CSE in the subject	
Not entered for GCE in the subject	351102 54.2%	134642 20.8%	485744 75.0%
Entered for GCE in the subject	146901 22.7%	14912 2.3%	161813 25.0%
	498003 76.9%	149554 23.1%	647557 100%

SUBJECT: HISTORY

	Not entered CSE in the subject	Entered for CSE in the subject	
Not entered for GCE in the subject	391948 60.5%	114044 17.6%	505992 78.1%
Entered for GCE in the subject	126833 19.6%	14732 2.3%	141565 21.9%
	518781 80.1%	128776 19.9%	647557 100%

SUBJECT: HOUSECRAFT

	Not entered CSE in the subject	Entered for CSE in the subject	
Not entered for GCE in the subject	510223 78.8%	87191 13.5%	597414 92.3%
Entered for GCE in the subject	43353 6.7%	6790 1.0%	50143 7.7%
	553376 85.5%	93981 14.5%	647557 100%

SUBJECT: MATHEMATICS

	Not entered CSE in the subject	Entered for CSE in the subject	
Not entered for GCE in the subject	183664 28.3%	262669 40.6%	446333 68.9%
Entered for GCE in the subject	170128 26.3%	31096 4.8%	201224 31.1%
	353792 54.6%	293765 45.4%	647557 100%

SUBJECT: MUSIC

	Not entered CSE in the subject	Entered for CSE in the subject	
Not entered for GCE in the subject	621918 96.0%	11532 1.8%	633450 97.8%
Entered for GCE in the subject	13859 2.2%	248 0.0%	14107 2.2%
	635777 98.2%	11780 1.8%	647557 100%

SUBJECT: PHYSICS

	Not entered CSE in the subject	Entered for CSE in the subject	
Not entered for GCE in the subject	463315 71.5%	80908 12.5.	544223 84.0%
Entered for GCE in the subject	91064 14.1%	12270 1.9%	103334 16.0%
	554379 85.6%	93178 14.4%	647557 100%

SUBJECT: RELIGIOUS STUDIES

	Not entered CSE in the subject	Entered for CSE in the subject	
Not entered for GCE in the subject	550545 85.0%	38396 5.9%	588941 90.9%
Entered for GCE in the subject	57385 8.9%	1231 0.2%	58616 9.1%
	607930 93.9%	39627 6.1%	647557 100%

SUBJECT: SOCIAL STUDIES

	Not entered CSE in the subject	Entered for CSE in the subject	
Not entered for GCE in the subject	617944 95.4%	25609 4.0.	643553 99.4%
Entered for GCE in the subject	3851 0.6%	153 0.0%	4004 0.6%
	621795 96.0%	25762 4.0%	647557 100%

SUBJECT: TECHNICAL DRAWING

	Not entered CSE in the subject	Entered for CSE in the subject	
Not entered for GCE in the subject	550537 85.0%	66699 10.3%	617236 95.3%
Entered for GCE in the subject	18242 2.8%	12079 1.9%	30321 4.7%
	568779 87.8%	78778 12.2%	647557 100%

SUBJECT: WOODWORK

	Not entered CSE in the subject	Entered for CSE in the subject	
Not entered for GCE in the subject	591009 91.3%	42234 6.5%	633243 97.8%
Entered for GCE in the subject	10594 1.6%	3720 0.6%	14314 2.2%
	601603 92.9%	45954 7.1%	647557 100%

Appendix F Estimated number (and proportions) of pupils in the 16+ age group who enter particular subjects in the CSE or the GCE sector before the end of the school year in which they have their sixteenth birthday—for boys and girls separately (1974)

The following is the order in which the subjects appear:

Art
Biology
Chemistry
Classical studies
Commerce
English language
English literature
English
French
German
Geography
History
Housecraft
Mathematics
Music
Physics
Religious studies
Social studies
Technical drawing
Woodwork

ART

	BOYS		
	Not Taking CSE	Taking CSE	
Not Taking GCE	239458 73.2%	55212 16.9%	294670 90.1%
Taking GCE	25767 7.9%	6490 2.0%	32257 9.9%
	265225 81.1%	61702 18.9%	326927 100%

	GIRLS		
	Not Taking CSE	Taking CSE	
Not Taking GCE	223563 69.7%	52640 16.4%	276203 86.1%
Taking GCE	36276 11.3%	8151 2.8%	44427 13.9%
	259839 81.0%	60791 19.0%	320630 100%

BIOLOGY

	BOYS		
	Not Taking CSE	Taking CSE	
Not Taking GCE	237760 72.7%	29340 9.0%	267100 81.7%
Taking GCE	55456 17.0%	4371 1.3%	59827 18.3%
	293216 89.7%	33711 10.3%	326927 100%

	GIRLS		
	Not Taking CSE	Taking CSE	
Not Taking GCE	161398 50.3%	76560 23.9%	237958 74.2%
Taking GCE	72342 22.6%	10330 3.2%	82672 25.8%
	233740 72.9%	86890 27½1%	320630 100%

CHEMISTRY

	BOYS					GIRLS		
	Not Taking CSE	Taking CSE				Not Taking CSE	Taking CSE	
Not Taking GCE	230594 70.5%	33056 10.1%	263650 80.6%		Not Taking GCE	274646 85.7%	18058 5.6%	292704 91.3%
Taking GCE	58141 17.8%	5136 1.6%	63277 19.4%		Taking GCE	24839 7.7%	3087 1.0%	27926 8.7%
	288735 88.3%	38192 11.7%	326927 100%			299485 93.4%	21145 6.6%	320630 100%

CLASSICAL
STUDIES

	BOYS					GIRLS		
	Not Taking CSE	Taking CSE				Not Taking CSE	Taking CSE	
Not Taking GCE	299481 91.6%	1348 0.4%	300829 92.0%		Not Taking GCE	300625 93.8%	1908 0.6%	302533 94.4%
Taking GCE	26098 8.0%	0 0	26098 8.0%		Taking GCE	17971 5.6%	126 0.0%	18097 5.6%
	325579 99.6%	1348 0.4%	326927 100%			318596 99.4%	2034 0.6%	320630 100%

COMMERCE

	BOYS					GIRLS		
	Not Taking CSE	Taking CSE				Not Taking CSE	Taking CSE	
Not Taking GCE	319509 97.7%	5510 1.7%	325019 99.4%		Not Taking GCE	293709 91.6%	22985 7.2%	316694 98.8%
Taking GCE	1517 0.5%	391 0.1%	1908 0.6%		Taking GCE	2719 0.8%	1217 0.4%	3936 1.2%
	321026 98.2%	5901 1.8%	326927 100%			296428 92.4%	24202 7.6%	320630 100%

ENGLISH

LANGUAGE

	BOYS					GIRLS		
	Not Taking CSE	Taking CSE				Not Taking CSE	Taking CSE	
Not Taking GCE	170938 52.3%	17586 5.4%	188524 57.7%		Not Taking GCE	159997 49.9%	14113 4.4%	174110 54.3%
Taking GCE	136627 41.8%	1776 0.5%	138403 42.3%		Taking GCE	144478 45.1%	2042 0.6%	146520 45.7%
	307565 94.1%	19362 5.9%	326927 100%			304475 95.0%	16155 5.0%	320630 100%

ENGLISH

LITERATURE

	BOYS					GIRLS		
	Not Taking CSE	Taking CSE				Not Taking CSE	Taking CSE	
Not Taking GCE	203879 62.3%	29280 9.0%	233159 71.3%		Not Taking GCE	174756 54.5%	34901 10.9%	209657 65.4%
Taking GCE	92075 28.2%	1693 0.5%	9376 28.⁻		Taking GCE	109649 34.2%	1324 0.4%	110973 34.6%
	295954 90.5%	30973 9.5%	32692 100%			284405 88.7%	36225 11.3%	320630 100%

ENGLISH

	BOYS					GIRLS		
	Not Taking CSE	Taking CSE				Not Taking CSE	Taking CSE	
Not Taking GCE	64049 19.6%	121762 37.3%	185811 56.9%		Not Taking GCE	52647 16.4%	117934 36.8%	170581 53.2%
Taking GCE	115858 35.4%	25258 7.7%	141116 43.1%		Taking GCE	118359 36.9%	31690 9.9%	150049 46.8%
	179907 55.0%	147020 45.0%	326927 100%			171006 53.3%	149624 46.7%	320630 100%

FRENCH

	BOYS					GIRLS		
	Not Taking CSE	Taking CSE				Not Taking CSE	Taking CSE	
Not Taking GCE	223139 68.3%	33752 10.3%	256891 78.6%	Not Taking GCE		194085 60.5%	50930 15.9%	245015 76.4%
Taking GCE	67014 20.5%	3022 0.9%	70036 21.4%	Taking GCE		69602 21.7%	6013 1.9%	75615 23.6%
	290153 88.8%	36774 11.2%	326927 100%			263687 82.2%	56943 17.8%	320630 100%

GERMAN

	BOYS					GIRLS		
	Not Taking CSE	Taking CSE				Not Taking CSE	Taking CSE	
Not Taking GCE	303971 93.0%	5932 1.8%	309903 94.8%	Not Taking GCE		288837 90.1%	9912 3.1%	298749 93.2%
Taking GCE	15887 4.8%	1137 0.4%	17024 5.2%	Taking GCE		20455 6.4%	1426 0.4%	21881 6.8%
	319858 97.8%	7069 2.2%	326927 100%			309292 96.5%	11338 3.5%	320630 100%

GEOGRAPHY

	BOYS					GIRLS		
	Not Taking CSE	Taking CSE				Not Taking CSE	Taking CSE	
Not Taking GCE	160666 49.1%	78421 24.0%	239087 73.1%	Not Taking GCE		190436 59.4%	56221 17.5%	246657 76.9%
Taking GCE	78864 24.2%	8976 2.7%	87840 26.9%	Taking GCE		68037 21.2%	5936 1.9%	73973 23.1%
	239530 73.3%	87397 26.7%	326927 100%			258473 80.6%	62157 19.4%	320630 100%

HISTORY

BOYS

	Not Taking CSE	Taking CSE	
Not Taking GCE	200309 61.3%	56569 17.3%	256878 78.6%
Taking GCE	62922 19.2%	7127 12.2%	70049 21.4%
	263231 80.5%	63696 19.5%	326927 100%

GIRLS

	Not Taking CSE	Taking CSE	
Not Taking GCE	191639 59.8%	57475 17.9%	249114 77.7%
Taking GCE	63911 19.9%	7605 2.4%	71516 22.3%
	255550 79.7%	65080 20.3%	320630 100%

HOUSECRAFT

BOYS

	Not Taking CSE	Taking CSE	
Not Taking GCE			
Taking GCE	NOT APPLICABLE		
			326927 100%

GIRLS

	Not Taking CSE	Taking CSE	
Not Taking GCE	183296 57.2	87191 27.2	270487 84.4
Taking GCE	43353 13.5%	6790 2.1%	50143 15.6%
	226649 70.7%	93981 29.3%	320630 100%

MATHEMATICS

BOYS

	Not Taking CSE	Taking CSE	
Not Taking GCE	82124 25.1%	129247 39.5%	211371 64.6%
Taking GCE	97741 29.9%	17815 5.5%	115556 35.4%
	179865 55.0%	147062 45.0%	326927 100%

GIRLS

	Not Taking CSE	Taking CSE	
Not Taking GCE	101540 31.7%	133422 41.6%	234962 73.3%
Taking GCE	72387 22.6%	13281 4.1%	85668 26.7%
	173927 54.3%	146703 45.7%	320630 100%

MUSIC

	BOYS		
	Not Taking CSE	Taking CSE	
Not Taking GCE	317441 97.1%	4484 1.4%	321925 98.5%
Taking GCE	4936 1.5%	66 0.0%	5002 1.5%
	322377 98.6%	4550 1.4%	326927 100%

	GIRLS		
	Not Taking CSE	Taking CSE	
Not Taking GCE	304477 95.0%	7048 2.2%	311525 97.2%
Taking GCE	8923 2.8%	182 0.0%	9105 2.8%
	313400 97.8%	7230 2.2%	320630 100%

PHYSICS

	BOYS		
	Not Taking CSE	Taking CSE	
Not Taking GCE	176092 53.8%	69489 21.3%	245581 75.1%
Taking GCE	71488 21.9%	9858 3.0%	81346 24.9%
	247580 75.7%	79347 24.3%	326927 100%

	GIRLS		
	Not Taking CSE	Taking CSE	
Not Taking GCE	287223 89.6%	11419 3.6%	298642 93.2%
Taking GCE	19576 6.1%	2312 0.7%	21988 6.8%
	306799 95.7%	13831 4.3%	320630 100%

RELIGIOUS

STUDIES

	BOYS		
	Not Taking CSE	Taking CSE	
Not Taking GCE	293888 89.9%	13287 4.1%	307175 94.0%
Taking GCE	19438 5.9%	314 0.1%	19752 6.0%
	313326 95.8%	13601 4.2%	326927 100%

	GIRLS		
	Not Taking CSE	Taking CSE	
Not Taking GCE	256657 80.1%	25109 7.8%	281766 87.9%
Taking GCE	37947 11.8%	917 0.3%	38864 12.1%
	294604 91.9%	26026 8.1%	320630 100%

SOCIAL
STUDIES

	BOYS					GIRLS		
	Not Taking CSE	Taking CSE				Not Taking CSE	Taking CSE	
Not Taking GCE	313319 95.8%	11968 3.7%	325287 99.5%		Not Taking GCE	304625 95.0%	13641 4.3%	318266 99.3%
Taking GCE	1628 0.5%	12 0.0%	1640 0.5%		Taking GCE	2223 0.7%	141 0.0%	2364 0.7%
	314947 96.3%	11980 3.7%	326927 100%			306848 95.7%	13782 4.3%	320630 100%

TECHNICAL
DRAWING

	BOYS					GIRLS		
	Not Taking CSE	Taking CSE				Not Taking CSE	Taking CSE	
Not Taking GCE	229907 70.3%	66699 20.4%	296606 90.7%		Not Taking GCE			
Taking GCE	18242 5.6%	12079 3.7%	30321 9.3%		Taking GCE	NOT APPLICABLE		
	248149 75.9%	78778 24.1%	326927 100%					320630 100%

WOODWORK

	BOYS					GIRLS		
	Not Taking CSE	Taking CSE				Not Taking CSE	Taking CSE	
Not Taking GCE	270379 82.7%	42234 12.9%	312613 95.6%		Not Taking GCE			
Taking GCE	10594 3.2%	3720 1.2%	14314 4.4%		Taking GCE	NOT APPLICABLE		
	280973 85.9%	45954 14.1%	326927 100%					320630 100%

Appendix G   Estimated numbers of pupils in the 16+ age group who entered specified CSE board subjects before the end of the school year in which they had their sixteenth birthday

ART

CSE BOARD	BOYS	GIRLS	TOTAL SAMPLE
11	1863	1998	3861
12	3444	2457	5901
13	5200	5512	10712
14	10065	8382	18447
15	2560	1616	4176
16	6744	6312	13056
17	8250	6501	14751
18	3339	4893	8232
19	2915	2541	5456
20	1560	1152	2712
21	4410	2212	6622
22	1332	630	1962
23	6510	12355	18865
24	3510	4230	7740
TOTAL	61702	60791	122493

BIOLOGY

CSE BOARD	BOYS	GIRLS	TOTAL SAMPLE
11	1998	4914	6912
12	2982	5901	8883
13	1820	5382	7292
14	3828	11847	15675
15	1712	3344	5056
16	4272	7416	11688
17	4191	10428	14619
18	2121	7539	9660
19	1199	3850	5049
20	1024	1944	2968
21	1890	3276	5166
22	1359	1719	3078
23	1450	13510	15960
24	2865	5820	8685
TOTAL	33711	86890	120601

CHEMISTRY

CSE BOARD	BOYS	GIRLS	TOTAL SAMPLE
11	1134	1242	2376
12	2226	1050	3276
13	4030	1430	5460
14	4587	1518	6105
15	1568	928	2496
16	4056	1968	6024
17	6369	3003	9372
18	2940	1848	4788
19	1188	1221	2409
20	1360	560	1920
21	2114	364	2478
22	1098	567	1665
23	2905	3675	6580
24	2370	1770	4140
TOTAL	37945	21144	59089

CLASSICAL STUDIES	CSE BOARD	BOYS	GIRLS	TOTAL SAMPLE
	11	–	–	–
	12	–	–	–
	13	–	–	–
	14	0	462	462
	15	0	32	32
	16	360	216	576
	17	0	0	0
	18	84	336	420
	19	33	11	44
	20	32	32	64
	21	154	0	154
	22	–	–	–
	23	595	945	1540
	24	90	0	90
	TOTAL	1348	2034	3382

COMMERCE

CSE BOARD	BOYS	GIRLS	TOTAL SAMPLE
11	810	459	1269
12	42	1155	1197
13	208	2808	3016
14	132	4290	4422
15	256	1280	1536
16	168	984	1152
17	1815	3168	4983
18	273	1428	1701
19	396	1496	1892
20	424	696	1120
21	756	952	1709
22	126	1071	1197
23	315	3605	3920
24	180	810	990
TOTAL	5901	24202	30103

ENGLISH (CSE)	CSE BOARD	BOYS	GIRLS	TOTAL SAMPLE
	11	6858	6777	13635
	12	189	126	315
	13	11284	12064	23348
	14	18348	20790	39138
	15	7856	5680	13536
	16	13800	13704	27504
	17	9240	6501	15741
	18	9870	12978	22848
	19	5412	6083	11495
	20	4480	3992	8472
	21	8386	7770	16156
	22	5175	3069	8244
	23	14385	22785	37170
	24	9630	9210	18840
	TOTAL	124913	131529	256442

ENGLISH LANGUAGE	CSE BOARD	BOYS	GIRLS	TOTAL SAMPLE
	11	–	–	–
	12	9429	9324	18753
	13	–	–	–
	14	–	–	–
	15	–	–	–
	16	–	–	–
	17	9933	6831	16764
	18	–	–	–
	19	–	–	–
	20	–	–	–
	21	–	–	–
	22	–	–	–
	23	–	–	–
	24	–	–	–
	TOTAL	19362	16155	35517

ENGLISH LITERATURE	CSE BOARD	BOYS	GIRLS	TOTAL SAMPLE
	11	-	-	-
	12	5124	6237	11361
	13	-	-	-
	14	-	-	-
	15	2976	2752	5728
	16	-	-	-
	17	9339	6402	15741
	18	4410	8484	12894
	19	-	-	-
	20	24	40	64
	21	-	-	-
	22	-	-	-
	23	8785	11725	20510
	24	315	585	900
	TOTAL	30973	36225	67198

ENGLISH

CSE BOARD	BOYS	GIRLS	TOTAL SAMPLE
11	6858	6777	13635
12	9618	9702	19320
13	11336	12090	23426
14	18381	20790	39171
15	8864	6384	15248
16	13800	13704	27504
17	19041	13431	32472
18	10101	13566	23667
19	5412	6083	11495
20	4488	4008	8496
21	8386	7770	16156
22	5175	3069	8344
23	15855	22785	38640
24	9705	9465	19170
TOTAL	147020	149624	296644

FRENCH

CSE BOARD	BOYS	GIRLS	TOTAL SAMPLE
11	4320	5049	9369
12	3150	4032	7182
13	4160	6812	10972
14	4356	7920	12276
15	1488	1008	2496
16	1944	3768	5712
17	3168	5841	9009
18	2457	5439	7896
19	1507	2508	4015
20	1032	1152	2184
21	1470	2380	3850
22	1107	1629	2736
23	3150	4830	7980
24	3465	4575	8040
TOTAL	36774	56943	93717

GERMAN

CSE BOARD	BOYS	GIRLS	TOTAL SAMPLE
11	837	864	1701
12	336	714	1050
13	962	1846	2808
14	1419	3498	4917
15	192	208	400
16	384	552	936
17	825	495	1320
18	231	756	987
19	264	396	660
20	200	208	408
21	224	266	490
22	315	270	585
23	700	980	1680
24	180	285	465
TOTAL	7069	11338	18407

GEOGRAPHY

CSE BOARD	BOYS	GIRLS	TOTAL SAMPLE
11	5265	2808	8073
12	5565	4431	9996
13	7774	5798	13572
14	11814	8844	20658
15	5568	2816	8384
16	8736	6456	15192
17	10725	5511	16236
18	5943	5964	11907
19	3982	4114	8096
20	1904	1064	2968
21	3542	2632	6174
22	3609	1539	5148
23	7105	5950	13055
24	5865	4230	10095
TOTAL	87397	62157	149554

HISTORY

CSE BOARD	BOYS	GIRLS	TOTAL SAMPLE
11	3645	2592	6237
12	4284	4515	8799
13	5408	6500	11908
14	6270	5577	11847
15	4672	3200	7872
16	5616	6048	11664
17	9240	7821	17061
18	4746	6930	11676
19	2750	3168	5918
20	1624	1416	3040
21	3136	3584	6720
22	3150	1494	4644
23	5180	7000	12180
24	3975	5235	9210
TOTAL	63696	65080	128776

HOUSECRAFT	CSE BOARD	BOYS	GIRLS	TOTAL SAMPLE
	11	-	4536	-
	12	-	6153	-
	13	-	7982	-
	14	-	13596	-
	15	-	4112	-
	16	-	9024	-
	17	-	9669	-
	18	-	8631	-
	19	-	4224	-
	20	-	2640	-
	21	-	3612	-
	22	-	1557	-
	23	-	12180	-
	24	-	6135	-
	TOTAL	-	93981	-

MATHEMATICS	CSE BOARD	BOYS	GIRLS	TOTAL SAMPLE
	11	9180	9639	18819
	12	10185	9597	19782
	13	12688	12584	25272
	14	18381	20955	39336
	15	8432	6752	15184
	16	13608	11352	24960
	17	18084	14718	32802
	18	8715	13923	22638
	19	5962	7293	13255
	20	4408	3032	7440
	21	9638	6832	15470
	22	4581	3096	7677
	23	13580	15155	28735
	24	10620	11775	22395
	TOTAL	147062	146703	293765

MUSIC

CSE BOARD	BOYS	GIRLS	TOTAL SAMPLE
11	162	243	405
12	483	693	1176
13	312	884	1196
14	1089	1287	2376
15	176	304	480
16	576	912	1488
17	396	1023	1419
18	189	399	588
19	187	517	704
20	248	296	544
21	308	28	336
22	144	99	243
23	70	140	210
24	210	405	615
TOTAL	4550	7230	11780

PHYSICS

CSE BOARD	BOYS	GIRLS	TOTAL SAMPLE
11	3537	459	3996
12	3465	945	4410
13	7774	676	8450
14	10758	1551	12309
15	4768	576	5344
16	7656	1176	8832
17	13398	2574	15972
18	4200	1113	5313
19	2915	462	3377
20	2456	304	2760
21	3724	308	4032
22	2466	252	2718
23	8435	2205	10640
24	3795	1230	5025
TOTAL	79347	13831	93178

RELIGIOUS
STUDIES

CSE BOARD	BOYS	GIRLS	TOTAL SAMPLE
11	405	1053	1458
12	903	2247	3150
13	546	3328	3874
14	627	2343	2970
15	1984	1920	3904
16	576	4008	4584
17	2145	2574	4719
18	252	2289	2541
19	990	803	1793
20	792	976	1768
21	2058	896	2954
22	513	324	837
23	385	1435	1820
24	1425	1830	3255
TOTAL	13601	26026	39627

SOCIAL STUDIES	CSE BOARD	BOYS	GIRLS	TOTAL SAMPLE
	11	405	243	648
	12	798	462	1260
	13	858	338	1196
	14	1254	4191	5445
	15	–	–	–
	16	672	1368	2040
	17	0	99	99
	18	–	–	–
	19	440	759	1199
	20	416	432	848
	21	3654	3038	6692
	22	1368	954	2322
	23	980	805	1785
	24	840	855	1695
	TOTAL	11685	13544	25229

	CSE BOARD	BOYS	GIRLS	TOTAL SAMPLE
TECHNICAL DRAWING	11	2943	-	-
	12	4788	-	-
	13	6240	-	-
	14	12045	-	-
	15	5760	-	-
	16	7248	-	-
	17	12045	-	-
	18	4494	-	-
	19	2607	-	-
	20	2360	-	-
	21	2688	-	-
	22	2475	-	-
	23	9475	-	-
	24	3600	-	-
	TOTAL	78778	-	-

WOODWORK

CSE BOARD	BOYS	GIRLS	TOTAL SAMPLE
11	1674	-	-
12	2667	-	-
13	3718	-	-
14	3960	-	-
15	4560	-	-
16	5088	-	-
17	6567	-	-
18	1848	-	-
19	2222	-	-
20	1512	-	-
21	2646	-	-
22	1377	-	-
23	4830	-	-
24	3285	-	-
TOTAL	45954		

Appendix H   Means and standard deviations of Test 100 scores for those pupils in the 16+ age group who had entered particular subject examinations with particular CSE boards before the end of the school year in which they had their sixteenth birthday
(* denotes less than 50 candidates)

ART

CSE BOARD	BOYS		GIRLS		TOTAL SAMPLE	
	Mean	s.d.	Mean	s.d.	Mean	s.d.
11	29.13	9.47	26.85	9.19	27.95	9.36
12	30.18	11.02	27.95	10.71	29.25	10.93
13	30.79	11.57	29.32	10.77	30.03	11.18
14	29.89	11.15	27.62	9.79	28.86	10.60
15	27.35	9.88	24.69	7.57	26.32	9.13
16	32.01	12.42	28.12	10.05	30.13	11.49
17	29.00	9.90	26.72	9.09	27.99	9.61
18	29.32	11.58	26.78	10.61	27.81	11.07
19	29.15	10.97	28.60	10.40	28.89	10.70
20	25.56	10.71	25.86	8.49	25.69	9.82
21	23.21	10.54	22.72	9.73	23.05	10.27
22	29.38	12.18	30.04	9.75	29.59	11.44
23	29.54	11.79	27.01	11.35	27.89	11.55
24	29.52	11.19	27.28	10.05	28.30	10.63
TOTAL	28.84	12.27	26.81	11.46	27.81	11.97

BIOLOGY

CSE BOARD	BOYS		GIRLS		TOTAL SAMPLE	
	Mean	s.d.	Mean	s.d.	Mean	s.d.
11	36.37	10.45	28.89	7.54	31.05	9.12
12	36.18	11.18	30.56	10.16	32.45	10.83
13	37.51	10.62	29.92	8.88	31.84	9.90
14	33.05	11.79	30.22	9.66	30.91	10.28
15	30.89	6.68	26.02	8.21	27.67	8.67
16	34.72	10.12	29.75	8.87	31.57	9.64
17	36.81	11.64	28.46	9.24	30.86	10.66
18	37.95	9.89	29.59	9.45	31.43	10.15
19	33.42	9.92	30.22	8.99	30.98	9.31
20	29.53	11.82	27.12	9.92	27.95	10.66
21	32.05	12.34	25.95	8.90	28.18	10.69
22	34.43	10.94	30.00	10.76	31.95	11.05
23	33.40	11.89	29.84	9.85	30.39	10.26
24	35.81	10.38	30.74	10.35	32.41	10.62
TOTAL	34.46	12.12	28.88	11.02	30.46	11.56

CHEMISTRY

CSE BOARD	BOYS		GIRLS		TOTAL SAMPLE	
	Mean	s.d.	Mean	s.d.	Mean	s.d.
11	39.59	9.48	32.60	7.84	35.94	9.30
12	40.79	12.19	41.88	12.53	41.14	12.27
13	41.45	11.15	40.47	10.06	41.19	10.86
14	40.15	12.44	36.52*	12.76*	39.24	12.59
15	36.44	9.90	34.62	10.16	35.76	10.00
16	37.09	10.42	34.70	11.14	36.31	10.69
17	39.35	11.13	34.32	8.67	37.74	10.65
18	37.63	10.02	40.05	10.89	38.57	10.41
19	39.35	10.99	36.07	9.67	37.68	10.45
20	36.30	12.39	30.54	9.48	34.62	11.89
21	33.18	12.35	29.96*	8.23*	32.71	11.87
22	35.82	10.18	32.07	11.26	34.55	10.68
23	40.91	12.25	33.62	11.84	36.84	12.53
24	44.16	11.00	38.40	10.02	41.70	10.95
TOTAL	38.69	12.92	35.35	12.32	37.32	13.32

CLASSICAL STUDIES

CSE BOARD	BOYS		GIRLS		TOTAL SAMPLE	
	Mean	s.d.	Mean	s.d.	Mean	s.d.
11	–	–	–	–	–	–
12	–	–	–	–	–	–
13	–	–	–	–	–	–
14	–	–	33.50*	8.47*	33.50*	8.47*
15	–	–	35.50*	3.53*	35.50*	3.53*
16	39.06*	7.84*	31.22*	6.22*	35.75*	8.36*
17	–	–	–	–	–	–
18	42.50*	4.20*	38.62*	11.74*	39.40*	10.68*
19	50.66*	5.77*	42.00*	0.00*	48.50*	6.40*
20	46.00*	17.37*	35.50*	9.43*	40.75*	14.10*
21	40.81*	8.88*	–	–	40.81*	8.88*
22	–	–	–	–	–	–
23	34.11*	12.81*	28.18*	8.09*	30.47*	10.45*
24	56.16*	9.60*	–	–	56.16*	9.60*
TOTAL	42.11	11.04	33.69	7.60	38.05	11.66

COMMERCE

CSE BOARD	BOYS		GIRLS		TOTAL SAMPLE	
	Mean	s.d.	Mean	s.d.	Mean	s.d.
11	36.10*	10.72*	26.47*	7.02*	32.61*	10.56*
12	39.50*	9.19*	27.49	7.82	27.91	8.09
13	35.00*	9.44*	29.37	8.58	29.76	8.72
14	40.50*	16.68*	32.54	9.85	32.78	10.11
15	34.87*	10.86*	26.28	7.72	27.71	8.86
16	33.00*	12.84*	28.36*	7.95*	29.04*	8.81*
17	34.34	9.05	28.16	7.86	30.14	8.81
18	38.15*	11.56*	28.19	10.84	29.79	11.49
19	30.75	9.22	28.87	7.10	29.26	7.60
20	31.84	12.21	27.79	8.27	29.32	10.10
21	24.03	9.72	24.30	7.48	24.18	8.51
22	36.50*	8.97*	28.06	10.78	28.95	10.89
23	32.00*	8.09*	28.14	9.87	28.45	9.77
24	39.33*	10.81*	26.14	9.42	28.54	10.88
TOTAL	34.70	4.27	27.82	11.61	29.21	10.83

ENGLISH
(CSE)

CSE BOARD	BOYS		GIRLS		TOTAL SAMPLE	
	Mean	s.d.	Mean	s.d.	Mean	s.d.
11	32.46	10.97	27.64	8.86	30.07	10.25
12	21.77*	5.76*	15.16*	5.45*	19.13	6.39
13	35.21	11.15	28.53	8.99	31.76	10.62
14	31.55	11.34	27.27	9.09	29.28	10.42
15	27.07	8.89	24.39	6.99	25.95	8.25
16	33.09	11.38	27.57	9.15	30.34	10.68
17	31.20	9.56	25.21	7.40	28.73	9.21
18	33.31	11.21	26.78	9.69	29.60	10.86
19	30.89	9.99	26.55	8.36	28.59	9.41
20	29.74	10.48	25.40	8.59	27.70	9.88
21	24.63	10.84	24.02	9.99	24.34	10.44
22	30.36	10.99	25.55	9.64	28.57	10.75
23	32.66	11.07	29.07	10.63	30.46	10.94
24	31.71	11.07	26.65	9.43	29.23	10.60
TOTAL	30.55	13.41	25.73	12.68	28.17	13.07

ENGLISH
LANGUAGE

CSE BOARD	BOYS		GIRLS		TOTAL SAMPLE	
	Mean	s.d.	Mean	s.d.	Mean	s.d.
11	-	-	-	-	-	-
12	32.44	11.26	27.93	10.15	30.20	10.95
13	-	-	-	-	-	-
14	-	-	-	-	-	-
15	-	-	-	-	-	-
16	-	-	-	-	-	-
17	33.01	11.03	27.83	7.68	30.90	10.12
18	-	-	-	-	-	-
19	-	-	-	-	-	-
20	-	-	-	-	-	-
21	-	-	-	-	-	-
22	-	-	-	-	-	-
23	-	-	-	-	-	-
24	-	-	-	-	-	-
TOTAL	32.89	10.94	27.87	9.23	30.64	10.25

ENGLISH LITERATURE	CSE BOARD	BOYS		GIRLS		TOTAL SAMPLE	
		Mean	s.d.	Mean	s.d.	Mean	s.d.
	11	-	-	-	-	-	-
	12	34.53	12.35	30.54	11.30	32.34	11.94
	13	-	-	-	-	-	-
	14	-	-	-	-	-	-
	15	33.58	10.19	27.28	8.31	30.55	9.84
	16	-	-	-	-	-	-
	17	32.49	10.89	27.56	7.68	30.48	10.00
	18	37.61	11.60	27.75	10.81	31.12	12.02
	19	-	-	-	-	-	-
	20	34.33*	21.93*	33.80*	9.78*	34.00*	13.86*
	21	-	-	-	-	-	-
	22	-	-	-	-	-	-
	23	35.03	11.23	28.93	9.49	31.54	10.70
	24	38.52*	6.93*	34.41*	11.40*	35.85	10.19
	TOTAL	34.99	9.55	29.26	7.92	31.79	9.54

ENGLISH

CSE BOARD	BOYS		GIRLS		TOTAL SAMPLE	
	Mean	s.d.	Mean	s.d.	Mean	s.d.
11	32.46	10.97	27.64	8.86	30.07	10.25
12	32.41	11.35	28.45	11.00	30.42	11.34
13	35.28		28.59	9.09	31.83	10.69
14	31.53	11.18	27.27	9.09	29.27	10.42
15	28.55	9.89	25.33	7.55	27.20	9.12
16	33.09	11.38	27.57	9.15	30.34	10.68
17	32.10	10.34	26.58	7.65	29.82	9.71
18	33.85	11.73	27.48	10.28	30.20	11.37
19	30.89	9.99	26.55	8.36	28.59	9.41
20	20.79	10.55	25.48	8.66	27.76	9.93
21	24.63	10.84	24.02	9.99	24.34	10.44
22	30.36	10.99	25.55	9.64	28.57	10.75
23	34.09	11.75	29.07	10.63	31.13	11.37
24	31.74	11.04	26.74	9.38	29.27	10.55
TOTAL	31.65	11.98	26.89	10.71	29.24	11.62

FRENCH

CSE BOARD	BOYS		GIRLS		TOTAL SAMPLE	
	Mean	s.d.	Mean	s.d.	Mean	s.d.
11	43.11	10.65	37.14	9.76	39.89	10.59
12	43.55	10.02	34.35	9.83	38.39	10.90
13	44.53	10.88	35.85	9.59	39.14	10.93
14	44.46	11.58	35.20	9.14	38.49	10.99
15	37.80	10.87	30.69	9.33	34.93	10.82
16	43.41	10.88	36.78	8.74	39.04	10.01
17	39.34	10.77	35.26	10.70	36.69	10.88
18	43.11	11.04	37.22	10.97	39.05	11.32
19	38.86	10.34	33.26	9.01	35.36	9.93
20	39.67	11.92	31.02	8.93	35.10	11.30
21	35.49	12.22	30.31	8.83	32.29	10.54
22	43.76	12.28	35.53	10.20	38.86	11.79
23	32.80	10.55	35.48	10.51	38.76	11.26
24	46.41	11.26	36.73	9.86	40.90	11.52
TOTAL	41.79	14.45	34.66	12.28	37.50	13.50

GERMAN

CSE BOARD	BOYS		GIRLS		TOTAL SAMPLE	
	Mean	s.d.	Mean	s.d.	Mean	s.d.
11	46.58*	10.49*	40.84*	9.45*	43.66	10.31
12	48.68*	14.82*	40.00*	12.78*	42.78	13.93
13	46.78*	12.09*	36.50	11.08	40.02	12.39
14	46.86*	11.02*	38.45	9.31	40.87	10.52
15	42.33*	11.08*	38.38*	10.49*	40.28*	10.74*
16	44.68	15.58	37.47	11.07	40.43	13.41
17	42.84*	9.69*	37.60*	11.98*	40.87*	10.77*
18	53.63*	9.04*	38.02*	11.01	41.68*	12.43*
19	44.08*	9.02*	38.52*	9.04*	40.75	9.37
20	45.28*	13.88*	33.76*	10.30*	39.41	13.39
21	33.43*	8.89*	30.47*	10.61*	31.82*	9.83*
22	45.62*	10.49*	36.16*	9.62*	41.26	11.09
23	43.60*	13.78*	37.67*	12.71*	40.14*	13.35*
24	48.58*	6.70*	40.68*	9.95*	43.74*	9.55*
TOTAL	44.90	13.88	37.32	12.69	40.21	13.72

GEOGRAPHY

CSE BOARD	BOYS		GIRLS		TOTAL SAMPLE	
	Mean	s.d.	Mean	s.d.	Mean	s.d.
11	32.52	11.25	29.52	8.05	31.48	10.33
12	33.37	9.40	29.80	9.84	31.79	9.75
13	36.68	11.03	31.34	9.70	34.40	10.80
14	35.73	13.15	31.70	9.93	34.00	12.04
15	28.62	8.90	26.40	7.92	27.87	8.64
16	31.95	9.62	28.93	9.11	30.67	9.52
17	32.72	10.66	29.59	8.75	31.65	10.15
18	34.71	10.48	32.54	10.42	33.62	10.50
19	32.31	9.71	29.90	8.85	31.09	9.35
20	30.26	10.38	29.54	9.92	30.00	10.21
21	26.83	9.89	25.29	8.67	26.17	9.41.
22	32.02	12.01	31.21	10.87	31.78	11.68
23	35.23	10.88	29.24	10.70	32.50	11.19
24	34.91	11.68	32.50	10.54	33.90	11.27
TOTAL	32.89	12.34	29.58	11.46	31.50	12.13

HISTORY

CSE BOARD	BOYS		GIRLS		TOTAL SAMPLE	
	Mean	s.d.	Mean	s.d.	Mean	s.d.
11	33.25	9.66	34.60	10.48	33.81	10.01
12	34.83	10.42	29.16	9.70	31.92	10.44
13	34.82	10.09	31.18	9.50	32.83	9.93
14	32.48	11.61	31.01	10.69	31.79	11.20
15	28.97	9.20	25.62	7.62	27.61	8.74
16	33.52	10.20	29.12	8.98	31.24	9.83
17	32.60	10.87	28.31	8.88	30.63	10.22
18	35.25	11.43	29.37	11.30	31.76	11.70
19	31.15	9.04	28.85	9.12	29.97	9.14
20	29.25	10.99	27.23	10.37	28.31	10.74
21	24.31	9.71	24.21	9.51	24.26	9.59
22	31.35	11.48	29.83	10.49	30.86	11.18
23	33.06	10.89	31.14	9.67	31.95	10.24
24	33.75	10.57	30.24	10.19	31.76	10.50
TOTAL	32.17	11.68	29.38	10.24	30.71	11.19

HOUSECRAFT

CSE BOARD	BOYS		GIRLS		TOTAL SAMPLE	
	Mean	s.d.	Mean	s.d.	Mean	s.d.
11	–	–	–	–	–	–
12	–	–	28.47	11.55	–	–
13	–	–	–	–	–	–
14	–	–	–	–	–	–
15	–	–	25.03	7.13	–	–
16	–	–	–	–	–	–
17	–	–	26.54	8.36	–	–
18	–	–	26.98	10.19	–	–
19	–	–	–	–	–	–
20	–	–	26.08	9.01	–	–
21	–	–	–	–	–	–
22	–	–	–	–	–	–
23	–	–	26.12	9.33	–	–
24	–	–	27.53	9.29	–	–
TOTAL	–	–	27.55	9.58	–	–

MATHEMATICS

CSE BOARD	BOYS		GIRLS		TOTAL SAMPLE	
	Mean	s.d.	Mean	s.d.	Mean	s.d.
11	34.44	10.64	33.39	9.63	33.90	10.14
12	34.14	10.41	31.54	10.80	32.88	10.67
13	36.54	10.97	33.21	9.99	34.88	10.62
14	33.63	11.14	31.62	9.74	32.56	10.46
15	30.19	9.35	28.22	8.55	29.31	9.05
16	34.45	10.61	31.65	9.30	33.18	10.13
17	31.91	9.99	30.56	8.76	31.30	9.48
18	36.89	10.37	32.14	10.49	33.97	10.69
19	32.78	10.07	30.01	8.83	31.25	9.50
20	31.88	11.47	29.01	8.99	30.71	10.62
21	26.02	11.61	26.91	9.89	26.41	10.89
22	33.72	11.21	33.17	11.33	33.50	11.25
23	35.48	11.22	33.35	10.18	34.36	10.73
24	35.11	11.85	31.52	11.18	33.22	11.63
TOTAL	33.33	11.77	31.12	11.15	32.19	11.63

MUSIC

CSE BOARD	BOYS		GIRLS		TOTAL SAMPLE	
	Mean	s.d.	Mean	s.d.	Mean	s.d.
11	38.00*	15.07*	42.44*	12.08*	40.66*	13.02*
12	36.34*	11.15*	27.21*	13.23*	30.96	13.12
13	42.91*	11.68*	32.70*	9.77*	35.36*	11.13*
14	33.18*	9.39*	32.20*	9.34*	32.65	9.31
15	23.36*	6.59*	30.89*	7.23*	28.13	7.81
16	31.79*	10.75*	27.94*	9.12*	29.43	9.88
17	38.08*	9.23*	32.09*	9.53*	33.76*	9.72*
18	31.55*	9.09*	29.68*	9.71*	30.28*	9.39*
19	35.52*	12.17*	31.10*	10.41*	32.38	10.98
20	31.19*	9.87*	30.51*	10.30*	30.82	10.04
21	29.13*	14.09*	30.50*	6.36*	29.25*	13.53*
22	34.87*	10.22*	38.72*	8.88*	36.44*	9.71*
23	31.00*	7.07*	37.50*	13.77*	35.33*	11.62*
24	30.35*	11.07*	28.48*	7.60*	29.12*	8.84*
TOTAL	33.58	11.61	32.26	6.22	32.55	9.52

PHYSICS

CSE BOARD	BOYS		GIRLS		TOTAL SAMPLE	
	Mean	s.d.	Mean	s.d.	Mean	s.d.
11	37.84	10.02	35.88*	8.20*	37.62	9.82
12	39.47	10.51	39.15*	11.15*	39.40	10.63
13	38.79	10.74	43.46*	15.65*	39.16	11.25
14	38.30	11.88	43.95*	8.21*	39.02	11.62
15	31.39	9.64	34.44	10.06	31.72	9.72
16	34.82	10.45	39.18*	10.11*	35.40	10.50
17	33.70	10.31	33.26	9.60	33.63	10.19
18	38.76	9.86	44.39	9.61	39.94	10.06
19	35.51	11.10	35.95*	9.73*	35.57	10.91
20	33.87	11.49	33.76*	10.36*	33.86	11.35
21	28.10	11.99	32.36*	7.37*	28.42	11.75
22	35.44	10.45	37.03*	11.49*	35.59	10.54
23	36.80	11.47	36.46	10.98	36.73	11.35
24	39.48	11.43	38.70	11.14	39.29	11.35
TOTAL	35.85	11.59	37.80	11.74	36.09	11.78

RELIGIOUS
STUDIES

CSE BOARD	BOYS		GIRLS		TOTAL SAMPLE	
	Mean	s.d.	Mean	s.d.	Mean	s.d.
11	37.73*	8.20*	30.64*	7.85*	32.61	8.47
12	32.13*	8.71*	26.59	8.78	28.18	9.08
13	47.90*	15.95*	31.99	11.74	33.72	13.63
14	34.42*	10.38*	29.57	8.86	30.60	9.35
15	28.14	8.50	24.85	7.05	26.52	7.97
16	32.16*	13.56*	25.75	8.54	26.56	9.51
17	29.36	9.61	25.87	8.17	27.46	8.99
18	26.91*	8.06*	27.64	9.81	27.57	9.62
19	49.11	17.81	32.27	11.87	41.57	17.53
20	30.39	11.94	25.79	9.52	27.85	10.89
21	23.26	11.18	29.46	8.46	25.14	10.80
22	33.36	13.52	22.88*	10.55*	29.31	13.41
23	25.63*	10.71*	29.17*	9.41*	28.42	9.70
24	46.18	14.02	40.01	11.21	42.71	12.86
TOTAL	33.15	14.04	28.44	10.81	29.81	12.81

SOCIAL
STUDIES

CSE BOARD	BOYS		GIRLS		TOTAL SAMPLE	
	Mean	s.d.	Mean	s.d.	Mean	s.d.
11	31.93	5.94	27.66	7.36	30.33*	6.69*
12	22.89*	8.55*	21.45*	9.38*	22.36	8.81
13	22.42*	7.39*	17.38*	5.83*	21.00*	7.29*
14	28.02*	10.02*	26.63	9.25	26.95	9.42
15	-	-	-	-	-	-
16	30.17	9.91	26.07	7.70	27.42	8.65
17	-	-	26.66	3.78	26.66*	3.78*
18	-	-	-	-	-	-
19	27.45*	9.85*	23.66	7.15	25.05	8.40
20	27.28	11.90	24.05	9.39	25.64	10.77
21	23.02	9.91	20.88	8.59	23.05	9.39
22	26.83	10.34	25.40	10.26	26.24	10.31
23	18.17*	8.21*	16.17*	5.39*	17.27	7.09
24	25.80	8.84	24.78	8.35	25.29	9.57
TOTAL	25.47	8.04	23.21	10.53	24.50	8.88

TECHNICAL DRAWING	CSE BOARD	BOYS		GIRLS		TOTAL SAMPLE	
		Mean	s.d.	Mean	s.d.	Mean	s.d.
	11	34.57	11.09	-	-	-	-
	12	35.79	10.92	-	-	-	-
	13	36.74	10.54	-	-	-	-
	14	34.99	11.93	-	-	-	-
	15	30.16	10.00	-	-	-	-
	16	33.05	11.18	-	-	-	-
	17	33.08	10.19	-	-	-	-
	18	36.01	11.95	-	-	-	-
	19	30.30	9.75	-	-	-	-
	20	30.49	10.52	-	-	-	-
	21	29.11	11.52	-	-	-	-
	22	34.55	12.16	-	-	-	-
	23	34.05	11.48	-	-	-	-
	24	21.70	10.84	-	-	-	-
	TOTAL	33.31	12.15	-	-	-	-

WOODWORK

CSE BOARD	BOYS		GIRLS		TOTAL	
	Mean	s.d.	Mean	s.d.	Mean	s.d.
11	34.59	10.73	-	-	-	-
12	31.59	11.47	-	-	-	-
13	31.50	11.75	-	-	-	-
14	32.60	11.39	-	-	-	-
15	26.66	8.47	-	-	-	-
16	30.53	10.28	-	-	-	-
17	30.07	11.37	-	-	-	-
18	33.31	10.03	-	-	-	-
19	29.07	9.95	-	-	-	-
20	28.36	10.14	-	-	-	-
21	26.89	11.22	-	-	-	-
22	32.13	12.31	-	-	-	-
23	32.73	11.96	-	-	-	-
24	29.04	9.95	-	-	-	-
TOTAL	30.79	10.13	-	-	-	-

Appendix I   Mean Test 100 scores for candidates by CSE board and by subject in 1968

CSE BOARD	SUBJECT										
	Art	Biol.	Chem.	Eng.	Fren.	Geog.	Hist.	Maths	Phys.	R.E.	T.D.
11	–	35.6	45.8	36.7	45.2	37.3	37.3	41.6	41.4	36.7	–
12	–	35.3	40.3	34.8	41.2	36.4	35.3	28.5	35.7	35.3	–
13	–	37.7	–	36.4	43.9	38.2	36.5	39.5	41.4	37.2	–
14	–	37.7	42.9	37.3	41.2	39.1	36.5	38.5	42.1	36.7	–
15	–	35.0	41.6	33.2	40.3	35.2	33.5	37.4	37.1	33.0	–
16	–	38.1	48.9	38.7	45.7	38.6	40.1	42.1	40.4	34.5	–
17	–	38.4	41.9	36.2	43.7	36.6	36.6	39.4	41.7	25.8	–
18	–	37.1	41.3	36.8	45.0	38.1	37.6	38.2	39.9	35.7	–
19	–	38.1	42.9	36.6	45.8	40.1	40.7	41.5	47.2	36.0	–
20	–	37.3	42.8	34.6	41.5	37.0	37.6	37.3	41.6	30.9	–
21	–	32.1	36.0	30.5	41.3	31.5	31.3	33.7	35.6	33.3	–
22	–	38.0	43.9	33.8	42.8	37.1	33.6	40.5	41.1	31.8	–
23	–	41.5	47.1	42.0	48.3	41.7	40.7	41.1	45.2	42.3	–
24	–	41.0	41.0	37.4	46.3	36.7	37.1	40.3	40.5	34.4	–

–   indicates information not available

Appendix J   Mean Test 100 scores for candidates by CSE board and by subject in 1973

CSE BOARD	SUBJECT									
	Art	Biol.	Chem.	Eng.	Fren.	Geog.	Hist.	Maths	Phys.	T.D.
11	30.9	35.5	42.3	33.9	43.6	36.2	37.1	39.7	38.4	39.6
12	30.6	32.9	39.9	31.7	40.8	33.8	32.6	33.6	36.6	34.5
13	33.4	34.7	44.5	33.8	39.6	36.7	36.8	36.5	39.6	37.7
14	35.7	34.7	43.0	35.1	41.2	37.1	35.9	36.4	39.9	35.8
15	27.7	33.0	40.1	29.4	38.7	30.0	31.4	34.0	37.6	32.0
16	32.2	34.0	37.1	32.9	41.2	32.9	33.0	36.0	39.3	36.0
17	34.1	34.4	40.0	32.4	42.9	33.5	34.9	35.4	39.7	34.8
18	32.6	36.9	44.7	32.8	42.1	33.8	35.1	37.8	41.4	35.6
19	31.2	36.4	41.7	31.5	41.2	34.8	34.3	36.3	39.4	36.1
20	28.8	34.2	37.3	29.1	37.5	32.4	30.8	31.9	36.7	33.7
21	30.0	33.1	38.8	28.6	39.3	31.3	33.2	32.3	36.0	30.5
22	26.6	33.3	36.9	29.3	40.7	34.1	33.0	35.0	38.2	31.9
23	33.9	36.0	45.3	34.8	41.9	36.1	38.4	39.3	41.8	39.6
24	33.7	35.6	42.6	34.1	43.2	36.0	37.5	36.5	40.9	35.2

Appendix K   Estimated numbers of pupils in the 16+ age group who entered specified GCE board subjects before the end of the school year in which they had their sixteenth birthday

ART

GCE BOARD	BOYS	GIRLS	TOTAL SAMPLE
01	6664	8072	14736
02	8453	9561	18014
03	5625	10365	15990
04	2756	6088	8844
05	2128	1536	3664
06	2329	–	–
07	5795	7413	13208
08	0	231	231
TOTAL	32257	44427	76684

BIOLOGY

GCE BOARD	BOYS	GIRLS	TOTAL SAMPLE
01	6481	15616	22097
02	16474	17278	33752
03	13950	25087	39037
04	6374	10200	16574
05	4299	2656	6955
06	6765	2273	9038
07	5450	8775	14225
08	63	1449	1512
TOTAL	59827	82672	142499

CHEMISTRY

GCE BOARD	BOYS	GIRLS	TOTAL SAMPLE
01	7616	3736	11352
02	23157	6792	29949
03	13279	9707	22986
04	6070	3623	9693
05	2634	960	3594
06	5066	720	5786
07	5450	1961	7411
08	21	441	462
TOTAL	140441	149200	289641

CLASSICS

GCE BOARD	BOYS	GIRLS	TOTAL SAMPLE
01	2150	4422	6572
02	9696	5217	14913
03	4034	4616	8650
04	1205	2479	3684
05	768	672	1440
06	7847	553	8400
07	311	211	522
08	0	357	357
TOTAL	26098	18097	44195

COMMERCE

GCE BOARD	BOYS	GIRLS	TOTAL SAMPLE
01	162	618	780
02	–	–	–
03	429	521	950
04	66	762	828
05	256	208	464
06	–	–	–
07	983	1715	2698
08	42	189	231
TOTAL	1908	3936	5844

ENGLISH LANGUAGE

GCE BOARD	BOYS	GIRLS	TOTAL SAMPLE
01	13382	18748	32130
02	41617	37362	78979
03	29211	38293	67504
04	12840	13939	26779
05	8176	5360	13536
06	14542	3172	17714
07	17123	22436	39559
08	147	462	609
TOTAL	138403	146520	284923

ENGLISH LITERATURE	GCE BOARD	BOYS	GIRLS	TOTAL SAMPLE
	01	11577	19384	30961
	02	28220	27808	56028
	03	20535	27445	47980
	04	8349	15601	23950
	05	6347	4448	10795
	06	11962	2927	14889
	07	7287	12523	19810
	08	0	1092	1092
	TOTAL	93768	110973	204741

ENGLISH	GCE BOARD	BOYS	GIRLS	TOTAL SAMPLE
	01	17585	24567	42152
	02	43658	39918	83576
	03	30742	40057	70799
	04	13549	20146	33695
	05	8395	5776	14171
	06	17793	4006	21799
	07	18708	27032	45740
	08	147	1344	1491
	TOTAL	141116	150049	291165

FRENCH

GCE BOARD	BOYS	GIRLS	TOTAL SAMPLE
01	4668	14602	19270
02	21439	17376	38815
03	15647	20405	36052
04	5388	10456	15844
05	2912	2320	5232
06	13986	2233	16219
07	6621	8809	15430
08	42	630	672
TOTAL	70036	75615	145651

GERMAN

GCE BOARD	BOYS	GIRLS	TOTAL SAMPLE
01	1538	5072	6610
02	5707	4162	9869
03	3735	5635	9370
04	1093	3367	4460
05	666	480	1146
06	2526	335	2861
07	1465	2669	4134
08	0	378	378
TOTAL	17024	21881	38905

GEOGRAPHY

GCE BOARD	BOYS	GIRLS	TOTAL SAMPLE
01	11107	14530	25637
02	24565	13553	38118
03	19301	20697	39998
04	8963	10955	19918
05	4490	2352	6842
06	6567	1771	8338
07	13108	9122	22230
08	0	1029	1029
TOTAL	87840	73973	161813

HISTORY

GCE BOARD	BOYS	GIRLS	TOTAL SAMPLE
01	9535	10252	19787
02	17924	14943	32867
03	16110	21590	37700
04	7112	10852	17964
05	3424	2864	6288
06	7302	1433	8735
07	8945	7639	16584
08	0	1680	1680
TOTAL	70049	71516	141565

HOUSECRAFT

GCE BOARD	BOYS	GIRLS	TOTAL SAMPLE
01	–	6140	–
02	–	9843	–
03	–	15072	–
04	–	4655	–
05	–	2704	–
06	–	0	–
07	–	12360	–
08	–	336	–
TOTAL	–	50143	–

MATHEMATICS

GCE BOARD	BOYS	GIRLS	TOTAL SAMPLE
01	11085	14226	25311
02	33375	19454	52829
03	22420	23331	45751
04	9686	11273	20959
05	5658	2656	8314
06	10679	1758	12437
07	17448	11205	28653
08	336	882	1218
TOTAL	115556	85668	201224

MUSIC

GCE BOARD	BOYS	GIRLS	TOTAL SAMPLE
01	768	1411	2179
02	1474	2147	3621
03	1240	2470	3710
04	450	876	1326
05	368	608	976
06	401	704	1105
07	313	632	945
08	0	126	126
TOTAL	5002	9105	14107

PHYSICS

GCE BOARD	BOYS	GIRLS	TOTAL SAMPLE
01	9208	3513	12721
02	26357	5068	31425
03	17163	7481	24644
04	8272	2751	11023
05	4053	624	4677
06	6373	780	7153
07	10041	1877	11918
08	0	273	273
TOTAL	81346	21988	103334

RELIGIOUS
STUDIES

GCE BOARD	BOYS	GIRLS	TOTAL SAMPLE
01	1550	4511	6061
02	4506	5936	10442
03	9724	16059	25783
04	131	3863	3994
05	1216	1616	2832
06	289	865	1154
07	1965	3860	5825
08	0	357	357
TOTAL	19752	38864	58616

SOCIAL
STUDIES

GCE BOARD	BOYS	GIRLS	TOTAL SAMPLE
01	-	-	-
02	-	-	-
03	336	512	848
04	-	-	-
05	-	-	-
06	-	-	-
07	1263	1852	3115
08	-	-	-
TOTAL	1545	2459	4004

TECHNICAL DRAWING	GCE SAMPLE	BOYS	GIRLS	TOTAL SAMPLE
	01	3134	-	-
	02	5260	-	-
	03	3894	-	-
	04	2730	-	-
	05	1856	-	-
	06	344	-	-
	07	13720	-	-
	08	105	-	-
	TOTAL	30321	-	-

WOODWORK	GCE BOARD	BOYS	GIRLS	TOTAL SAMPLE
	01	-	-	-
	02	5814	-	-
	03	1968	-	-
	04	1237	-	-
	05	1504	-	-
	06	66	-	-
	07	3669	-	-
	08	0	-	-
	TOTAL	14314	-	-

Appendix L   Means and standard deviations of Test 100 scores for those pupils in the 16+ age group who had entered particular subjects with particular GCE boards before the end of the school year in which they had their sixteenth birthday

(* denotes less than 50 candidates)

ART

GCE BOARD	BOYS		GIRLS		TOTAL SAMPLE	
	Mean	s.d.	Mean	s.d.	Mean	s.d.
01	40.31	15.04	43.01	12.42	41.79	13.73
02	44.97	12.93	39.08	12.45	41.85	13.01
03	44.67	12.09	40.19	11.32	41.77	11.79
04	48.88	15.16	43.41	12.33	45.11	13.66
05	37.64	12.68	32.84	11.06	35.63	12.26
06	54.17	12.94	47.82*	13.01*	52.21	13.29
07	40.64	12.17	36.55	10.93	38.34	11.67
08	–	–	40.00*	15.36*	40.00*	15.36*
TOTAL	43.35	13.63	40.61	12.53	41.77	13.07

BIOLOGY

GCE BOARD	BOYS		GIRLS		TOTAL SAMPLE	
	Mean	s.d.	Mean	s.d.	Mean	s.d.
01	51.17	11.87	48.52	11.47	49.30	11.69
02	53.19	10.47	44.89	11.61	48.94	11.82
03	51.43	11.18	45.94	11.35	47.90	11.65
04	51.91	11.99	46.38	11.21	48.51	11.82
05	47.38	12.67	39.62	11.28	44.42	12.73
06	53.86	11.42	48.93	12.93	52.62	12.01
07	46.34	10.99	40.51	10.44	42.74	11.03
08	36.66*	4.06*	40.02	11.19	39.88	11.01
TOTAL	51.88	11.76	45.50	11.70	48.18	12.14

CHEMISTRY

GCE BOARD	BOYS		GIRLS		TOTAL SAMPLE	
	Mean	s.d.	Mean	s.d.	Mean	s.d.
01	55.04	10.49	54.77	10.33	54.95	10.44
02	57.07	10.40	49.18	11.70	55.28	11.21
03	55.85	10.17	51.44	11.48	53.99	10.96
04	54.78	11.85	57.02	9.63	55.62	11.12
05	52.49	9.81	46.38	11.39	50.86	10.61
06	60.01	8.69	55.61*	12.86*	59.46	9.42
07	50.62	10.66	50.53	11.61	50.60	10.92
08	49.00*	0.00*	49.42*	9.22*	49.40*	9.00*
TOTAL	49.89	12.92	42.91	12.53	46.29	13.19

CLASSICS

GCE BOARD	BOYS		GIRLS		TOTAL SAMPLE	
	Mean	s.d.	Mean	s.d.	Mean	s.d.
01	55.99	9.93	57.13	8.43	56.75	10.13
02	61.41	9.26	51.70	12.44	58.01	11.46
03	58.34	10.15	53.44	11.73	55.73	11.29
04	58.84*	7.02*	57.32	10.63	57.82	10.51
05	54.14*	10.94*	45.83*	11.63*	50.26	12.00
06	57.30	9.63	62.99*	13.18*	57.67	10.00
07	60.00*	9.39*	50.76*	10.25*	56.27*	10.74*
08	-	-	40.70*	13.24*	40.70*	13.24*
TOTAL	59.96	10.30	54.43	11.89	57.70	11.31

COMMERCE

GCE BOARD	BOYS		GIRLS		TOTAL SAMPLE	
	Mean	s.d.	Mean	s.d.	Mean	s.d.
01	46.77*	12.73*	38.13*	6.78*	39.92	9.06
02	-	-	-	-	-	-
03	43.30*	8.19*	42.02*	7.37*	42.60*	7.77*
04	21.00*	1.00*	38.60*	9.01*	37.20*	9.88*
05	42.56*	8.64*	26.76*	4.91*	35.48*	10.66*
06	-	-	-	-	-	-
07	36.55	10.73	33.81	10.73	34.81	10.81
08	43.00*	11.13*	37.33*	11.71*	38.36*	11.79*
TOTAL	39.20	11.20	36.15	10.02	37.15	10.52

ENGLISH LANGUAGE

GCE BOARD	BOYS		GIRLS		TOTAL SAMPLE	
	Mean	s.d.	Mean	s.d.	Mean	s.d.
01	46.17	12.56	46.03	12.26	46.09	12.44
02	51.34	12.59	41.03	12.36	46.47	13.50
03	49.77	12.19	44.77	11.86	46.94	12.25
04	49.04	12.94	43.80	12.59	46.31	13.03
05	44.65	12.42	37.64	10.65	41.87	12.24
06	53.82	11.16	44.35	14.35	52.13	12.34
07	43.61	11.29	30.69	10.55	39.69	11.40
08	44.85*	9.58*	35.22*	11.12*	37.55*	11.53*
TOTAL	50.01	12.91	43.00	12.52	46.41	13.18

ENGLISH LITERATURE

GCE BOARD	BOYS Mean	s.d.	GIRLS Mean	s.d.	TOTAL SAMPLE Mean	s.d.
01	50.26	12.09	48.08	11.74	48.90	11.92
02	53.78	11.04	44.44	11.42	49.14	12.17
03	52.10	11.60	46.11	11.54	48.67	11.94
04	46.96	11.58	46.46	12.12	46.64	11.93
05	45.90	12.56	39.08	11.15	43.09	12.46
06	53.25	11.84	46.43	14.02	51.91	12.59
07	47.83	11.29	41.93	11.17	44.10	11.57
08	-	-	40.28	12.18	40.28	12.18
TOTAL	51.71	12.15	45.48	11.95	48.34	12.43

ENGLISH

GCE BOARD	BOYS Mean	s.d.	GIRLS Mean	s.d.	TOTAL SAMPLE Mean	s.d.
01	47.76	13.14	46.40	12.07	46.97	12.66
02	51.17	12.46	41.22	12.31	46.42	13.41
03	49.91	12.23	44.81	11.79	47.03	12.24
04	49.12	12.89	44.94	12.53	46.62	12.84
05	44.72	12.41	38.21	10.79	42.07	12.20
06	54.04	11.27	44.52	13.80	52.29	12.34
07	43.98	11.38	38.05	11.06	40.48	11.56
08	44.85*	9.58*	39.96	12.21	40.45	12.07
TOTAL	49.88	12.91	42.88	12.53	46.27	13.19

FRENCH

GCE BOARD	BOYS		GIRLS		TOTAL SAMPLE	
	Mean	s.d.	Mean	s.d.	Mean	s.d.
01	54.26	9.06	51.82	10.39	52.41	10.26
02	57.35	9.59	49.08	10.26	53.65	10.71
03	55.32	10.67	49.54	11.08	52.05	11.27
04	57.76	11.24	50.92	11.52	53.24	11.88
05	52.51	11.36	42.08	10.90	47.89	12.30
06	56.35	10.68	48.00	13.94	55.20	11.55
07	51.27	12.03	42.61	10.95	46.32	12.20
08	48.00*	1.01*	47.06*	10.89*	47.12*	10.55*
TOTAL	56.45	10.97	49.22	11.38	52.69	11.75

GERMAN

GCE BOARD	BOYS		GIRLS		TOTAL SAMPLE	
	Mean	s.d.	Mean	s.d.	Mean	s.d.
01	57.05	8.44	52.00	10.91	53.17	10.94
02	60.17	9.35	50.78	9.77	56.21	10.60
03	58.09	7.39	52.50	10.84	54.73	10.60
04	59.86*	10.66*	54.75	9.81	56.00	10.26
05	52.48*	5.97	44.20*	9.24*	49.01	8.55
06	57.17	11.09	54.60*	13.05*	56.87	11.36
07	50.04	11.05	44.53	10.56	46.48	11.06
08	–	–	44.83*	10.39*	44.83*	10.39*
TOTAL	58.62	10.92	51.27	10.97	54.49	11.54

GEOGRAPHY

GCE BOARD	BOYS		GIRLS		TOTAL SAMPLE	
	Mean	s.d.	Mean	s.d.	Mean	s.d.
01	51.31	11.14	48.07	11.65	49.47	11.55
02	53.01	11.06	45.00	11.07	50.16	11.71
03	50.32	11.77	46.49	11.28	48.34	11.67
04	49.72	12.72	47.40	11.81	48.44	12.28
05	45.58	11.46	40.03	11.31	43.67	11.71
06	51.58	11.65	48.04	11.35	50.82	11.68
07	45.18	10.97	40.88	10.22	43.42	10.88
08	–	–	40.14*	12.22*	40.14*	12.22*
TOTAL	49.80	12.04	45.33	11.64	47.81	12.07

HISTORY

GCE BOARD	BOYS		GIRLS		TOTAL SAMPLE	
	Mean	s.d.	Mean	s.d.	Mean	s.d.
01	49.72	11.78	47.63	12.17	48.63	12.03
02	52.72	11.24	46.00	11.15	49.66	11.75
03	49.28	11.58	44.22	10.89	46.38	11.47
04	48.62	12.81	46.42	12.38	47.29	12.60
05	42.89	11.76	38.27	10.08	40.79	11.27
06	52.87	11.99	50.57	14.17	52.50	12.40
07	43.94	11.58	39.18	10.49	41.75	11.34
08	–	–	40.62	10.51	40.62	10.51
TOTAL	48.77	12.52	44.08	11.85	46.46	12.42

HOUSECRAFT

GCE BOARD	BOYS		GIRLS		TOTAL SAMPLE	
	Mean	s.d.	Mean	s.d.	Mean	s.d.
01	–	–	41.54	11.29	–	–
02	–	–	39.82	10.32	–	–
03	–	–	41.52	10.35	–	–
04	–	–	43.76	12.64	–	–
05	–	–	34.34	9.51	–	–
06	–	–	–	–	–	–
07	–	–	36.80	10.24	–	–
08	–	–	37.81*	10.10*	–	–
TOTAL	–	–	39.75	10.93	–	–

MATHEMATICS

GCE BOARD	BOYS		GIRLS		TOTAL SAMPLE	
	Mean	s.d.	Mean	s.d.	Mean	s.d.
01	51.84	11.25	50.98	9.95	51.36	10.88
02	54.88	10.66	48.93	10.23	52.69	10.89
03	51.53	11.36	48.25	10.96	49.86	11.28
04	53.59	11.92	50.84	11.36	51.65	11.66
05	48.38	11.51	43.07	11.19	46.68	11.67
06	52.35	10.33	51.45	12.35	52.22	10.65
07	46.83	9.87	43.97	9.41	45.71	9.80
08	44.25*	7.66*	45.59*	10.76*	45.22	10.02
TOTAL	53.36	12.06	48.86	11.04	51.57	11.87

MUSIC

GCE BOARD	BOYS		GIRLS		TOTAL SAMPLE	
	Mean	s.d.	Mean	s.d.	Mean	s.d.
01	50.89*	12.18*	50.26	8.08	50.48	9.73
02	52.01	11.14	47.62	11.97	49.41	11.84
03	54.45*	8.63*	45.52	9.72	48.51	11.12
04	56.72*	3.20*	52.09*	11.63*	53.66	11.32
05	47.65*	14.31*	42.26*	12.77*	44.29	13.62
06	56.60*	9.71*	40.15*	11.09*	46.12*	13.23*
07	43.86	8.34	40.60	10.45	41.68	9.91
08	-	-	42.00*	9.68*	42.00*	9.68*
TOTAL	51.36	11.66	46.37	11.61	48.32	11.88

PHYSICS

GCE BOARD	BOYS		GIRLS		TOTAL SAMPLE	
	Mean	s.d.	Mean	s.d.	Mean	s.d.
01	53.32	11.64	57.54	8.04	54.49	11.22
02	56.57	10.37	51.07	10.49	55.69	10.58
03	54.41	10.48	53.39	11.34	54.10	10.76
04	52.56	12.36	59.00	8.74	54.17	11.90
05	50.27	10.63	50.41*	10.64*	50.29	10.63
06	58.58	9.23	58.83*	11.96*	58.60	9.57
07	48.67	10.71	50.04	10.56	48.88	10.69
08	-	-	51.46*	7.85*	51.46*	7.85*
TOTAL	54.69	11.42	54.00	11.00	54.54	11.34

RELIGIOUS
STUDIES

GCE BOARD	BOYS		GIRLS		TOTAL SAMPLE	
	Mean	s.d.	Mean	s.d.	Mean	s.d.
01	43.92	13.27	44.10	11.28	44.05	11.82
02	52.12	11.44	38.90	10.99	44.61	12.96
03	50.73	12.87	43.21	11.62	46.05	12.64
04	53.28*	27.35*	44.70	12.18	44.98	12.21
05	43.44	12.96	35.01	9.08	38.63	11.69
06	55.01*	8.73*	43.37*	8.60*	46.29	10.00
07	38.55	11.95	37.58	9.44	37.91	10.36
08	–	–	39.00*	10.40*	39.00*	10.40*
TOTAL	50.25	13.00	42.54	11.88	45.14	12.79

SOCIAL
STUDIES

GCE BOARD	BOYS		GIRLS		TOTAL SAMPLE	
	Mean	s.d.	Mean	s.d.	Mean	s.d.
01	–	–	–	–	–	–
02	–	–	–	–	–	–
03	41.31*	9.09*	42.47*	8.77*	42.01*	8.91*
04	–	–	–	–	–	–
05	–	–	–	–	–	–
06	–	–	–	–	–	–
07	39.77	9.49	35.88	9.52	37.46	9.70
08	–	–	–	–	–	–
TOTAL	39.94	9.55	37.51	9.73	38.45	9.73

TECHNICAL DRAWING — GCE BOARD	BOYS Mean	s.d.	GIRLS Mean	s.d.	TOTAL SAMPLE Mean	s.d.
01	49.03	11.98	-	-	-	-
02	45.46	11.40	-	-	-	-
03	48.35	10.29	-	-	-	-
04	47.67	11.91	-	-	-	-
05	44.53	10.59	-	-	-	-
06	47.26*	12.72*	-	-	-	-
07	42.30	11.10	-	-	-	-
08	48.20*	6.70*	-	-	-	-
TOTAL	45.02	11.57	-	-	-	-

WOODWORK — GCE BOARD	BOYS Mean	s.d.	GIRLS Mean	s.d.	TOTAL SAMPLE Mean	s.d.
01	-	-	-	-	-	-
02	45.15	12.61	-	-	-	-
03	45.68	10.38	-	-	-	-
04	40.24	11.43	-	-	-	-
05	40.62	12.34	-	-	-	-
06	59.33*	5.28*	-	-	-	-
07	39.44	11.77	-	-	-	-
08	-	-	-	-	-	-
TOTAL	43.75	12.39	-	-	-	-

Appendix M   Mean Test 100 scores for candidates by GCE board and by subject in 1973

GCE BOARD	SUBJECT									
	Art	Biol.	Chem.	Eng.	Fren.	Geog.	Hist.	Maths	Phys.	T.D.
01	46.1	52.7	57.5	49.6	53.7	52.5	51.2	54.0	55.4	46.0
02	43.4	50.1	54.0	47.5	52.6	49.6	49.0	51.6	53.0	47.1
03	44.2	49.6	55.3	48.6	52.0	49.5	49.1	51.6	54.9	52.7
04	49.2	51.9	57.6	49.7	55.2	52.4	51.0	52.2	55.6	53.0
05	30.9	48.0	53.2	46.2	53.7	46.5	46.0	50.0	51.2	42.2
06	41.0	49.5	56.9	53.4	54.7	51.5	52.2	48.2	56.6	–
07	35.3	42.8	48.5	40.5	45.5	43.9	43.2	46.3	47.5	47.7
08	–	37.5	45.6	39.0	47.0	41.4	42.7	46.1	47.4	–

Major reports from ETRU in chronological order

1966
Schools Council. *The 1965 CSE Monitoring Experiment.* (Working Paper 6), Parts I and II. HMSO.

1968
Examinations and Tests Research Unit. *Highlights of the 1966 CSE Monitoring Experiment.* Slough: NFER.

1969
Nuttall, D. L., and Skurnik, L. S. *Examination and Item Analysis Manual.* Slough: NFER.
Skurnik, L. S., and Hall, J. *The 1966 CSE Monitoring Experiment.* (Schools Council Working Paper 21). HMSO.
Wood, R., and Skurnik, L. S. *Item Banking.* Slough: NFER.

1970
Skurnik, L. S., and Connaughton, I. M. *The 1967 CSE Monitoring Experiment.* (Schools Council Working Paper 30). Evans/Methuen Educational.

1971
Nuttall, D. L. *The 1968 CSE Monitoring Experiment.* (Schools Council Working Paper 34). Evans/Methuen Educational.
Nuttall, D. L. *Administrator's Manual for Science Attitude Questionnaire.* Slough: NFER.
Schools Council. *Question Banks: their Use in School Examinations.* (Examinations Bulletin 22). Evans/Methuen Educational.

1972
Nuttall, D. L., and Willmott, A. S. *British Examinations: Techniques of Analysis.* Slough: NFER.

1974
Fowles, D. E. *CSE: Two Research Studies.* (Schools Council Examinations Bulletin 28). Evans/Methuen Educational.

Nuttall, D. L., Backhouse, J. K., and Willmott, A. S. *Comparability of Standards between Subjects*. (Schools Council Examinations Bulletin 29). Evans/Methuen Educational.

Skurnik, L. S. *Monitoring Grade Standards in English*. (Schools Council Working Paper 49). Evans/Methuen Educational.

Willmott, A. S., and Fowles, D. E. *The Objective Interpretation of Test Performance: The Rasch Model Applied*. Slough: NFER.

1975

Duckworth, D. *The Experimental Certificate of Extended Education: Summer 1974*. Slough: NFER.

Hoste, R. and Bloomfield, B. *Continuous Assessment in the CSE: Opinion and Practice*. (Schools Council Examinations Bulletin 31). Evans/Methuen Educational.

Willmott, A. S., and Hall, C. G. W. *O Level Examined: the Effect of Question Choice*. (Schools Council Research Studies). Macmillan Education.

Willmott, A. S., and Nuttall, D. L. *The Reliability of Examinations at 16+*. (Schools Council Research Studies). Macmillan Education.

1976

Duckworth, D., and Hoste, R. *Question Banking: an Approach through Biology*. (Schools Council Examinations Bulletin 35). Evans/Methuen Educational.

1977

Bloomfield, B., Dobby, J. and Duckworth, D. *Mode Comparability in the CSE: a study of two subjects in two examining boards*. Schools Council Examinations Bulletin 36. Evans/Methuen Educational.

Willmott, A. S. *CSE and GCE Grading Standards: the 1973 Comparability Study*. (Schools Council Research Studies). Macmillan Education.

Reports submitted to the Schools Council during 1977

Bloomfield, B., Dobby, J. and Kendall, L. *Ability and Examinations at 16+*.

Dobby, J. L. and Duckworth, D. *Objective Assessment by means of Item Banking*. (Schools Council Examinations Bulletin 40). Evans/Methuen Educational.

Willmott, A. S. and Bloomfield, B. A. 'The 1974/1975 Comparability Study'.

Hickey, A. 'Qualifying for Higher Education under a New Examination System at 18+'.

References

Backhouse, J. K. (1973). Personal communication.

Butcher, H. J. (1970). *Human Intelligence : its Nature and Assessment.* Methuen.

Cochran, W. G. (1963). *Sampling Techniques* (2nd ed.). New York: John Wiley.

Department of Education and Science (1975). *Statistics of Education 1974*, vol. 1, *Schools.* HMSO.

Forrest, G. M. (1971). *Standards in Subjects at the Ordinary Level of the GCE, June 1970* (Occasional Publication No. 33). Manchester: Joint Matriculation Board.

Forrest, G. M. and Smith, G. A. (1972). *Standards in Subjects at the Ordinary Level of the GCE, June 1971* (Occasional Publication No. 34). Manchester: Joint Matriculation Board.

Guilford, J. P. (1965). *Fundamental Statistics in Psychology and Education* (4th ed.). New York: McGraw-Hill.

Guilford, J. P. (1967). *The Nature of Human Intelligence.* New York: McGraw-Hill.

Gulliksen, H. (1950). *Theory of Mental Tests.* New York: John Wiley.

Hall, C. G. W. (1975). Interim report on factorial structure of candidate attainment in public examinations—unpublished.

Hall, C. G. W. (1977). 'The structure of some educational abilities in public examinations at the sixteen plus age level in England and Wales'. D. Phil. thesis submitted through the University of Brunel Department of Education.

Heim, A. W. (1970). *Intelligence and Personality : the Assessment and Relationship.* Penguin.

Joint Matriculation Board (1972). *General Certificate of Education Regulations and Syllabuses 1974.* Manchester: Joint Matriculation Board.

Kendall, M. G., and Stuart, A. (1961). *The Advanced Theory of Statistics*, vol. II, *Inference and Relationship.* New York: Hafner.

Lord, F. M. and Novick, M. R. (1968). *Statistical Theories of Mental Test Scores.* Reading, Mass.: Addison-Wesley.

Nuttall, D. L. (1971). *The 1968 CSE Monitoring Experiment* (Schools Council Working Paper 34). Evans/Methuen Educational.

Nuttall, D. L., Backhouse, J. K. and Willmott, A. S. (1974). *Comparability of Standards Between Subjects* (Schools Council Examinations Bulletin 29). Evans/Methuen Educational.

Nuttall, D. L. and Willmott, A. S. (1972). *British Examinations: Techniques of Analysis.* Slough: NFER.

Schools Council (1966). *The 1965 CSE Monitoring Experiment* (Schools Council Working Paper 6, Parts I and II). HMSO.

Schools Council (1968). *Enquiry 1 : Young School Leavers.* HMSO.

Schools Council (1971). *A Common System of Examining at 16+* (Examinations Bulletin 23). Evans/Methuen Educational.

Schools Council (1975). *Examinations at 16+ : Proposals for the Future.* Evans/Methuen Educational.

Secondary School Examinations Council (1963). *The Certificate of Secondary Education: Some Suggestions for Teachers and Examiners.* (Examinations Bulletin No. 1). HMSO.

Skurnik, L. S. and Hall, J. (1969). *The 1966 CSE Monitoring Experiment.* (Schools Council Working Paper No. 21). HMSO.

Willmott, A. S. (1975). 'An analysis of GCE and CSE examination grades.' D. Phil. thesis submitted through the University of Oxford Department of Educational Studies.

Willmott, A. S. (1977). *GCE and CSE Grading Standards: the 1973 Comparability Study* (Schools Council Research Studies). Macmillan Education.

Willmott, A. S. and Bloomfield, B. A. (1977). 'The 1974/1975 comparability study.' Report to the Schools Council.

Willmott, A. S. and Nuttall, D. L. (1975). *The Reliability of Examinations at 16+.* (Schools Council Research Studies). Macmillan Education.